MOVED TO A NEW

MINDSET

MIN. DONNA MORRIS

MOVED TO A NEW

MINDSET

FREE FROM LIMITATIONS, REJECTIONS, AND FEARS

RESTORATION OF THE BREACH
WITHOUT BORDERS

West Palm Beach, Florida

MIN. DONNA M. MORRIS

MOVED TO A NEW MINDSET

Published by:
Restoration of the Breach without Borders
133 45th Street, Building A7
West Palm Beach, Florida 33407
restorativeauthor@gmail.com
Tele: (561) 388-2949

EBook Cover Design by:
Calbert Simson
divine.creativevillage@gmail.com

Editing done by:
Melisha Bartley-Ankle
melbarxtd@yahoo.com

Formatting and Publishing done by:
Sherene Morrison
Publisher.20@aol.com

Unless otherwise stated Scripture verses are quoted from the King James Version of the Bible.

DEDICATION

I want to dedicate this book to the memory of my mother, the late Elaine Bryan, it is also in tribute to her, whose unfailing love defined motherhood and was my first encounter with a wealthy mind, hard work and a woman of prayer who left God's fingerprints of grace on my life. You cannot be forgotten.

To everyone who is desirous of making that move of faith, breaking free from limitations in the mind and discovering the powerful purpose for their lives.

ACKNOWLEDGEMENTS

To God be all the Glory for making this book a reality. Gratefulness is flowing from my heart. *"This the Lord's doing, it is marvellous in our eyes" (Psalms 118:23).* The Lord has brought me through many circumstances, and I am so glad.

Thanks to The Holy Spirit who has been my source of divine inspiration, wisdom and strength. He continually teaches me in every phase of my life. Special Thanks to my wonderful husband, Donald Morris, for your love, encouragement, prayerful support and understanding. You gave me time and space to write. A lifelong partner like you makes the marital journey and destination worthwhile. You are a gift to my world. I am immensely grateful for my gifted son Damari Morris, who assisted in collating my writings. You are indeed a wonderful blessing from God, and I am truly grateful for you.

My family and all that will read this book, I say a big thank you.

Special thank you and appreciation to my friend Donna Ruddock-Rhoden, I acknowledge your prayerful influence in my life. Our journey in reading and studying God's Word together over the years has been a lifelong investment. I treasure your friendship, it is priceless.

Thank you to Reverend Conrad Thomas for your endorsement, your prayerful support and guidance is above and beyond measure. Being my Pastor, you have been a constant source of encouragement through your teaching and preaching the undiluted Word of God.

Melisha Bartley-Ankle, you are a gift in a special package, and I am grateful for your help along the journey. Your input and creative editing and endorsement on this book have been brilliant. Thank you.

Special appreciation to my friend Ambassador Pastor Robert Whyte, Thank you for your endorsement. Your wealth of kingdom insights and encouragement to pursue this phenomenal upgrade is of great value.

Rev Kevon Vidal, thank you for your obedience in delivering the Word that the Lord gave you. Glory to God, you came to preach and the power of God in you, brought deliverance to an impoverished mind. I pray you will continue to make yourself available to the Kingdom of God.

Continuous appreciation to my church Family at the Church of the United Missions (Beulah). I cherish your prayerful support and encouragement in all I do. I thank the Lord for you all.

Special Thank you and appreciation to Whole Life College, especially our wonderful Principal Pastor Rachel Thompson (affectionately called Pastor Shelly) and Miss Hope Fox. You have both been a great source of encouragement from the first day I entered the College. God bless you.

To my publisher Sherene Badjnuat - Morrison, who embraced this new way of thinking to carry out this task. Thank you for the follow up and excellent formatting and making sure this book becomes a reality.

Min Calbert Simpson, thank you so much for this beautiful graphic design for the book cover. It is indeed a Wow!

I must express my appreciation to Dr Vic and Rev May Victor, Founders of Institute of Marriage & Family Affairs (TIMFA). You teach and model skills that preserve and protect marriages as one of the best gifts from God. Thank you, Team

Victor, for empowering, training, and equipping marriage mentors around the world. Yes! I am empowered, and I have been encouraged to walk in Bold Exploits! And I intend to continue to do so.

I personally thank Reverend Leostone Morrison for writing the foreword for this book. It is not just acknowledgements but for your obedience to the Holy Spirit and for being a relentless source of encouragement to complete this project. Rev, you challenge me to keep going, and to maximize my fullest potential. Your words to me, "I am putting you out there." May God richly bless you.

I have been encouraged to walk in bold exploits and I purpose to continue to do so.

ENDORSEMENTS

There are many who have not yet discovered the art in tapping into the greatness that God has for them. However, Donna Morris in her book *Moved to a New Mindset*, has given her readers a practical guide in walking in God's divine plan which will lead to good success in every aspect of life. Read this masterpiece and your mind will definitely be renewed.

> -Missionary   Melisha Bartley-Ankle
> In His Presence
> 30 Days of Devotion, Declaration, Prayer & Reflection

*   *   *   *   *   *

The revelatory insight advanced by Ambassador Donna Morris in this literature is absolutely empowering. I believe this piece will provide an arsenal of strength for the reader to be catapulted to that dimension of manifestation, where the mind renewed and propelled in the right direction will bear much fruit by which our father will indeed be glorified. Feast your mind with this phenomenal upgrade and get ready for the introduction of the best version of yourself for such a time as this. It's your time for bold exploits!!

-Pastor Robert Whyte, JP
Senior Pastor, Bethel Embassy International Ministries

* * * * * *

"And be renewed in the spirit of your mind" (Ephesians 4:23).

This renewal is the work of the Holy Spirit, and it is so powerful.

I am thanking God for the passionate inspiration and drive through the Power of the Holy Spirit that stirred Min Donna Morris to write this book.

Moved to a New Mindset is indeed the Lord's doing.

 This book flows out of a committed mind that is renewed by the Word of God. Everyone can embark on this journey by freeing the mind from limitations and fears. However, with this freedom we must maximize potential, and opportunities presented to us.

This book impacted me deeply. It gives great insights that as you stand on the Word of God, you will be able to slay all Goliaths. Get ready for your new mindset. It is a blessing to the body of Christ.

Thank you, Minister Morris, for your obedience in sharing these highlights from your Mind Renewal Course.

-Reverend Conrad Thomas
Pastor,
Church of the United Missions (Beulah)
Kingston Jamaica

FOREWORD

An unfinished assignment is undiscovered wealth. Minister Donna Morris I say well done. You completed the Mind Renewal Nine Weeks Online Course and this beautiful book-**MOVED TO A NEW MINDSET** is the product of your first and final assignment. In this literature, you have captured your transformational journey which will be used to the betterment of others. It must never be considered a light gift when God uses your journey to impact the lives of others. Many lies have paraded as truth to the detriment of glorious possibilities.

To move to a new mindset requires truth, tenacity, and courage. It might include abandoning dogmas that you have held on to for centuries and embracing newly discovered truths. Minister Morris has carefully documented tools to advance you the reader into a new mindset. A powerful truth is you are your thoughts. The Bible says, 'as a man thinks so is he' (Proverbs 3:7). A new mindset equates a new person.

This book is not for information but for application. I encourage you to let the new mindset that awaits you, wait no more.

Move to a New MindSet and thank Minister Morris after.

-Rev Leostone Morrison
Author
Mind Renewal: Biblical Secrets to A Better You

TABLE OF CONTENTS

INTRODUCTION

The greatest war we will ever fight is what is in our Minds. However, it is certain that the wealth within our minds can be unlocked. Therefore, it is imperative that we should be renewing our minds with the Word of God every single day.

"And be not conformed to this world: but be ye transformed by the renewing of your mind, that ye may prove what is that good, and acceptable, and perfect, will of God." (Romans 12:2)

In this book, MOVED TO A NEW MINDSET provides highlights on my journey during the Mind Renewal Course through the Restoration of the Breach School. Glory be to God for our teacher and visionary Rev Leostone Morrison, and his obedience to partner with the Holy Spirit to write the book; *"Mind Renewal: Biblical Secrets to a Better You"*.

After completing the nine weeks Mind Renewal Course I thought I was only submitting my operational manual; but God flipped the script and showed me the clear path that he was leading me to write. Indeed, this is a setup from God. I have always known that it is in me to write, but never knew when or how it would happen. To God be the glory, the Lord of Hosts has orchestrated His plans and given me an expedited breakthrough.

The God of the open door shook my foundation and immediately all doors were opened and every one's bands were loosed". (Acts 16:26)

I am humbled to navigate through all the difficult seasons of my life and to know that God has kept me; I am just in awe of His love.

MOVED TO A NEW MINDSET is a living testimony of the Lord's doing and it is marvellous in our eyes. It is a good look! Yes! Yes! Refocus, renewed mindset, no limitations or fear. God has commanded this blessing, the shackles of my mind are loosed, chains fell off and my circumstances shifted. It is a liberating thought to know that God has made something beautiful in an unusual time in history. As things are changing in our world, God is still in the business of bringing transformation to the mind. Do not be discouraged by what you see, keep walking by faith and see where your belief will take you.

No ifs and or buts about it, my day of freedom is here! Thank you, Jesus! Certainly, all low grounds are rejected in Jesus' name, and I can extend my mind to a higher level of thinking.

As you review my writings through each module, you will receive encouragement and strength so you can move from where you are and experience victory today and beyond. It is imperative that you renew your mind, so you can walk free from limitations and fears. God is pulling you up and out, that you can enter that place of increase. Discover that it is possible to let go of your past, stand on the Word of God and slay every Goliath that seeks to hinder you from fulfilling your divine purpose.

Something new, fresh, and God-ordained is blossoming in my life, and it reminds me that God is faithful. *"Let us hold fast the profession of our faith without wavering; (for he is faithful that promised)" (Hebrews 10:23)*

Have an impactful read.

You are blessed.

CHAPTER 1

A WEALTHY OR AN IMPOVERISHED MIND?

Whatever challenges you are now facing, I want to offer you the hope that you can experience your time of mind renewal. I am thrilled for this Moving to a new mindset journey; it is one that keeps on moving. I felt the presence of the Lord, hovering over me each week as I completed my assignments. In essence, it was not like homework, but worship time and experiencing a new encounter with the Holy Spirit. With deep introspection, I am now discovering why I am here. When you begin to look at yourself from God's perspective, you will understand better that there is so much power in the mind. There is something very powerful about the Mind, however what you think has a huge impact on who you are becoming. As I

1

spend more time reading and studying the Word of God, I notice the desire to fast and pray steadily increases and my way of thinking also changes.

Do you believe and understand that the Mind is a powerful tool? Whether or not you are aware of the fact that it controls your life, it surely does. The Mind is vast and determines where you end up in life. What you regularly allow to dwell within your mind will eventually become a part of you. However, thinking on things that are lovely and praiseworthy will bring an expression of God's way of thinking. Experience has taught me that consistent deposit of God's Word in my mind has allowed me to let go of my way of thinking and embrace God's thinking. If you can get this truth deep within you it will change your life dramatically.

DO YOU WANT A WEALTHY OR AN IMPOVERISHED MIND?

2

Many people may have an impoverished mind and are not even aware of it. Evidence of doubt and fear is seen in this type of mindset. The apostle Paul emphasized in Ephesians 4:22-23 *"That ye put off concerning the former conversation the old man, which is corrupt according to the deceitful lusts; And be renewed in the spirit of your mind"*. This change of mindset requires great effort on our part.

It is imperative that we are renewed in the state of our minds.

There is so much in life that can create doubt. Understand that doubt will rob you of great mind wealth. What does the Bible say about doubt? *James 1:6: "But let him ask in faith, nothing wavering. For he that wavereth is like a wave of the sea driven with the wind and tossed "*. God wants you to exercise your faith and overcome the barriers of doubt. An impoverished mindset will cause you to waver in so much doubt that it traps you into thinking there are limits in your life and that you cannot achieve much. It is also referred to as a poor mindset. I have seen so many wealthy persons, living with a poverty mentality. It is not acceptable to believe that everything in your life is hard, or it is a struggle to make it through life. I have good news for you, if you are having any of those thoughts at any time, hear this truth: You can change your mindset. Especially in this day and age, your mindset has to be changed from the old way of thinking. Bear in mind, that even though ongoing challenges may still occur, it is possible to keep embracing the positive things in your life and letting go of the old mindset.

To break free from an impoverished mind you have to align your thoughts with the thoughts of God.

A wealthy mind is not afraid to go against the odds in life. Now is the time to act, you must activate your mind towards purpose. The concept of your mind been a forerunner is very powerful as it means that we will never tread the path where our minds have never gone. It must go before you, in the process of our thinking *as a mind thinketh in his heart, so is he. (Proverbs 23:7)*

In the concept of the Reservoir- Your mind must be opened, for example just as I stepped out by faith in doing this Mind Renewal course and to know that I am intentionally activating purpose. As a reservoir, my mind is being rejuvenated, this one is certain!! My mind reservoir will always have a desire to give of its content. I will not allow my mind reservoir to be polluted. Therefore, I will keep it open for the Lord, so He can minister His Word through me.... YES, there is a place in your reservoir for the Word of God!! Look at the treasure concerning you. Your mind reservoir has two uses, to receive and replenish. Having such knowledge, has the Word found a place in the reservoir of your life? Has your mind begun to STORE the Word so it can be used later?

Yes! It is possible. You Can have a wealthy mind!! Let the Word of God be your benchmark.

You can have good storage for the Lord to use!!!Importantly, it is not about how much Scripture verses you can recite - *BUT THE DEPTH OF THE WORD IN YOUR LIFE.*

A WEALTHY MIND CAN BE YOURS

How we measure ourselves in a competitive culture, against the need to outdo our peers in a bid to get across the finish line. However, there is a need to break free of your mindset. Each time you confess that you are not; this very thinking always goes ahead of you and produces results. According to Proverbs 18:21, *"Death and life is in the power of the tongue"*. See how important it is to pay attention to what you are confessing.

6

Irrespective of our background, we must renew our minds and improve our thinking.

It is possible for anyone to be great and excel, as the scripture says in Romans 4:17 *"we ought to call those things that are not as though they are".*

You do not have to get stuck in limitations, but it is possible for you to soar, just look at yourself for a moment. Are you experiencing a poor mindset right now and do you want that to change? Growth must be intentional; all this moving forward can only be navigated through a mind that is renewed. You can have a wealthy mind if you want, or you can choose to be stuck in an impoverished mindset. Today I rejoice over the fact that God has made it possible that if you seek Him with all your heart, you will find Him. (Jeremiah 29:13) You do not have to settle or compare with anyone; but you can step out by faith and expand the terrains of your mind and spirit. It is truly reassuring to know that you can

7

pull your mind from the familiar and step into the future. Whatever God has for you today can be yours. As long as your attitudes are transformed, you are in a different place from the crowd that surrounds you. Now is not the time to be COMPETITIVE!

I do agree that many people seek to compare themselves with others, whether through talents, gifting, and expectations. However, the more you pay attention to the fact that God has created you uniquely, you will be better able to overcome negative thinking and unleash the greatness inside you.

For a moment I reflected on the fact that for anyone to go to a higher dimension, you must learn to reject the commonality of life and push beyond the mediocre mind. At times you may look crazy to people around you! But amid the fact that you may be judged by others, you must persevere and do what must be done. People sometimes judge you for what you do, thank you Lord for this course!! Look what the Lord is doing right here in my life! When I look back at those seasons of my life where I have been judged by others or conspired against, it reveals to me that God had to unlock the wealth in my mind. I am beginning to see much clearer now that letting go of an impoverished mindset rests heavily on my willingness to pursue daily mind renewal...It is now imperative that I reject low grounds and stretch my mind to inhabit high frequencies.

MY EXPERIENCE WITH IMPOVERISHED MIND

I had experienced the same when I doubted God's provision concerning our home improvement project. Being afraid to step out in faith, fear and doubt caused me to walk by sight. Forgetting that God is my Resource Manager, I sought to strategize, save and work things on my own. However, if my mind were renewed, I would have understood the Power of God's promises towards me, moved at His command and received the overflow of God's divine provision.

ON A PERSONAL NOTE

On Sunday December 3, 2017, a visiting Pastor – Reverend Kevon Vidal from Worship House Restoration Ministries came to our church to minister the Word of God. As the Holy Spirit began to move upon the man of God, through the sermon that he was preaching, he called forth persons for prayer.

I was not among the lot that was called to the altar, but I was in dire need of a word. The prophetic word that came was that the Lord is about to do something new, and I need to step out by faith from where I was in my mind. As I write this testimony. I can still hear the voice of the

Pastor, saying **"Today is the day, New beginning. It is time to shift".** The fresh and potent anointing was evident in the service. I believe my faith was so lacking I thought I had to save money towards our home improvement before I could see it realized. It is really true that with a lack of knowledge we certainly perish. In fact, I believe I was perishing in my thoughts. Now I can say "But God." I was not even aware that if I do not show up in faith for the Promises of God's Word nothing will take place. It has been over two decades since my husband and I had purchased this quad and we did not do any home improvement. Things just looked bleakley and poor as if our God could not afford it…. Mercy LORD!!! But I continued to talk to God about the matter. On that day, it was a day for movements. For too long it had been declared no movement day in my mind. Now the time had come to move in faith. I realize that when you have an impoverished mindset, you are destined to live an average life, and remain trapped in limitations.

The promised word that was given to me through Reverend Vidal came from Psalms 89:34:

"My covenant will I not break nor alter the things which has gone out my lips."

The Word of the Lord came with such quickening power that it gave me an igniting shake up. This was an immediate move to a new mindset, Glory to God! One thing about the Word of God, once you receive it you have to move. It always gives you wisdom and clear directives. Can I hasten to tell you that on Monday I went to the National Housing Trust to inquire about a Home Improvement loan, and to my surprise I was more than qualified for it. The step of faith was so immediate, literally, the moment I received the Word of God, I was now able to walk in faith. At all times, you must receive God's word so you can act in faith. God's Word is fully loaded and is always ready to work on your behalf. Praise God, and it sure worked for me.

Distractions came in many shapes, but God came through nevertheless. At times it looked impossible, but God delivered on His promise. We are now able to open our beautiful front door and step out on the porch. All because of the Lord's doing. Look at God's goodness on display!! I encourage you to prepare to conquer those obstacles that have been encumbering your mind and be ready to embark on your journey of moving to a new mindset.

Today, I am living my promised word, a word that I never thought would have come to pass because of the challenges I faced during "The Between" (error on the building plan, delays in the processing of the loan, building permit expired, wrong work man), God had to realign some things, but through it all as the song writer

Andrae Crouch- said 'I have learned to trust in Jesus I have learned to depend upon His word". God is a covenant keeper, and He will always bring it to pass, no matter the setbacks, obstacles of all different sizes but I held on to the promises of God's Word.

As the Lord came forth the expansion became a reality. The Lord revealed this beautiful promise to seal the victory. *This is the Lord's doing and it is marvellous in our eyes. (Psalms 118:23).* **TO GOD BE THE GLORY!**

Impoverished minds really let us miss out on God's exceedingly, abundantly, above all blessings. In fact, it keeps you in the low grounds below the standard of God's victory package.

However, with my mind renewal experience, I learnt that I could have a wealthy mind. Receiving the Word of God is the first key to open the door of a wealthy mind. Another key is to live

God's promises and discover what He has in store for you. Therefore, instead of doubting and being fearful, you can walk in faith free from limitations and fears, rejecting the low ground. God promised to perfect everything that concerns you. The scripture expresses that truth in Psalms 138:8:

"The LORD will perfect that which concerns me: thy mercy, O LORD, endureth forever: forsake not the works of thine own hands."

GUARD YOUR MIND

As revealed earlier, your mind is a very powerful tool and by extension your life will be shaped by the way you think. In fact, Ephesians 4:23 says clearly that *"We ought to be renewed in the spirit of our minds"*. This means that we must always pay attention to the renewing of the mind, seeing that the thoughts that we allow to dwell in our minds will impact and shape our future. Bear in mind that the foundation of every human is their thought life. The scripture states it categorically by saying in Proverbs 23:7 that *"As a man thinketh in his heart so he is."* Once you take the time out to reflect on those thoughts, you will see the cause of your problems. This can be a wakeup call for many of you who do not understand that your world is ruled by your thoughts. You can begin to guard your mind by constantly infusing the Word of God in your mind. However, God has made it possible for us to regulate thoughts that come to our mind. The moment you begin to speak the Word of God through bold declaration, immediately you will be able to counteract all negative thought processes that come to your mind. Look at the ammunition that is made available to you through the Word of God. It is guaranteed to guard your mind. I have become so tired of thoughts of limitations dragging through my mind, in season and out of season, however the moment I begin to give myself to the study of the Word and do what it says, I realize that I put up a guard against impoverished thoughts. As long as your mind is fully guarded with The Sword of the Spirit which is the Word of God, (Ephesians 6:17) all negative thoughts have to depart. The truth is when your mind is guarded, it also prevents your tongue from uttering destructive words. Have you ever noticed that anyone who speaks negatively about life is usually known to have negative thoughts? Wholesome thoughts are beneficial to us and to others. In fact, your relationship with others will also improve when you are being renewed in the spirit of your mind. Pay attention to this, once you declare what the Word of God says about you, you will see your life transformed. Do not forget to guard your mind. It is a daily project. Now is the time to maximize the full potential of your mind and guard it as well.

MY THOUGHTS VS. WEALTHY THOUGHTS

17

I think, I am so fearful right now.

God says, *"I have not given you a spirit of fear.*

For I have not given you the spirit of fear but of power and of love and a sound mind." (2 Timothy 1:7).

I think it is impossible.

God says all things are possible.

"With God nothing shall be impossible." (Luke 1:37)

I think I can't.

God says you can do all things through Christ.

"I can do all things through Christ who strengthens me". (Philippians 4:13)

I think no one loves me.

God says I love you.

"For God so loved the world that he gave his only begotten Son, that whoever believes in him should not perish but have everlasting life." (John 3:16)

"The LORD hath appeared of old unto me, saying, Yea, I have loved thee with an everlasting love:

18

therefore, with lovingkindness have I drawn thee."
(Jeremiah: 31:3)

I think I am alone.

God says I will never leave you nor forsake you.

"Never will I leave you; never will I forsake."
(Hebrews 13:5)

I think I am ugly.

God says you are fearfully and wonderfully made

"I will praise thee; for I am fearfully and wonderfully made marvellous are thy works; and that my soul knoweth right well." (Psalm 139:14)

I think I am weak.

God says He is your refuge.

"God is our refuge and strength, a very present help in trouble." (Psalms 46:1)

I think I feel so burdened.

God says cast all your cares on Me.

"Cast all your cares upon him because he cares for you." (*1 Peter 5:7*)

I think I do not have enough faith.

God says I have given everyone the measure of faith.

"For by the grace given me I say to every one of you: Do not think of yourself more highly than he ought to think, but to think soberly, according as God hath dealt to every man the measure of faith." (*Romans 12:3*)

Now is the time to bask in the wealth of a mind that is filled with God's word. Embracing a mental shift is quite rewarding. It is my prayer that the Holy Spirit will enlighten you to refuse a mind that is impoverished and choose a wealthy mind. Do not delay, choose thoughts that will transform you.

CHAPTER 2
LET GO OF THE PAST

L *ife is a journey.* As we navigate life, we will experience challenges, disappointments and past hurts. Although we can learn from our past experiences, the fact of the matter is that they do not have to govern our lives and keep us trapped. Whether our past pain is close to the surface or hidden deep within our hearts, it has the potential to hold us back. The time has come to let go of the past, it is a choice that we have to make and only you alone can do that.

Some people will never move beyond the pain from their past, because they think that holding on to it is the right thing to do. However, it is impossible to move forward when painful emotions remain unaddressed. Regardless of how you may suppress it, or choose to avoid dealing with the past hurt, the only way out is to let it go. The hurts of the past will keep you from the joy of the present and the future. You must, therefore, understand that walking in denial concerning the past hurt, is very detrimental. Many times, persons pretend to be ok when in fact it is still there in the heart. Consequently, it is impossible to be genuinely happy when you are holding on to the past. It is inevitable that you will pay a very high price. Firstly, you will lose joy, and peace of mind. It is understandable that some persons may be afraid to confront the painful past. However, the reality is, for you to move forward, you need to admit you were hurt, face it, and share your testimony.

It is God's will that we move forward in our lives in the fulfilment of His purposes. One of the greatest deterrents of a bright future is to be trapped in the past. In Genesis 19:17, the Bible gives us an excellent example of someone who did not let go of the past. The Lord instructed Lot and his family while they were fleeing from Sodom that they should escape for their life and not to look back. In fact, when they were leaving the city of Sodom Lot's wife looked back, and she became a pillar of salt.

"Then the LORD rained upon Sodom and upon Gomorrah brimstone and fire from the LORD out of heaven; and he overthrew those cities, and all the plain, and all the inhabitants of the cities, and that which grew upon the ground. But his wife looked back from behind him, and she became a pillar of salt". (*Genesis 19:24-26*)

Lot's wife was unable to separate herself from her former life, and because her eyes were fastened on her past, she was left behind. When you let go of the past, then you will be able to experience the fullness of life. Her progress in life had abruptly halted because she refused to let go. Are you holding on to the past, refusing to let go? We all tend to hold onto things that have happened in the past, looking back is never a good thing! Leave those past hurts behind you. In a manner of speaking, you could say that it is like a heavy baggage on our backs. God is the only one that can release you of the load, however you have to do your part in choosing to let go. As soon as you release the baggage you will feel lighter and free. Having held on to the pain for a very long time it eventually becomes a part of you.

Sometimes the past is so painful that letting go may even feel impossible. Instead of focusing on the past, focus on the victories ahead. You would be so amazed at the number of persons that have held onto the past and unforgiveness has blotted out.

Thinking about what may have happened to you in the past will impress on you to share the story with anyone who will listen, because you just need an available outlet. Thankfully, I have learned through the Mind Renewal Course that not everyone who listens to your story wants you to break free. Be careful who you share your past with. Despite what you may think, God is always willing to free you from it, the moment you decide to let go of the past. You are on your way to freedom.

God's best will never be achieved if you hold unto the pain of the past. Every time you try to move on here comes that old tape replaying hurts, wounds, something in the present always brings it back. In other words, one minute you are in the present and the next you are stuck in the past, feeling the hurt all over again. Contrary to what many persons may think, let me reassure you that it does not matter if you have been victimized physically, spiritually, or emotionally there is hope for you. God is still able to do a work of healing in your life. You can let go of all bitterness and resentment.

25

As Ephesians 3:20 expresses, *Our God is able to do all things, he is able to do more than we can ask, think or imagine.* It is possible to learn from the past without living in it.

BE FORGIVING: IT FREES YOU

The Apostle Paul wrote in 2 Corinthians 2:11 that we are not to let Satan *"Take advantage of us; for we are not ignorant of his devices."* Many times he gets the advantage over people who are not aware of how he works. It is time for God's people to know the tactics of the Devil. One of the enemy's greatest weapons is unforgiveness. He seeks to nullify the blessings and victories in the life of believers from being committed to God. The Lord has shown me that part of the devil's tactics is to keep God's people ignorant of His Word. Throughout the Bible, great emphasis is placed on the matter of Forgiveness: Let us look at a few scriptures on the warning given.

"For if ye forgive men their trespasses, your heavenly Father will also forgive you: But if ye forgive not men their trespasses, neither will your Father forgive your trespasses". (*Matthew 6:14-15*)

……." Forgive, and ye shall be forgiven." Luke 6:37

"And forgive us our debts, as we for/give our debtors". (*Matthew 6:12*)

Unfortunately, some believers are not taking heed to the Word of God, in regard to *walking in forgiveness. Here is how James put it: "Be ye doers of God's Word and not hearers only, deceiving your own selves".* In fact, Many Christians would want God's forgiveness, but they are not willing to forgive those who have offended them. Yet this is the only way they can receive forgiveness. Ultimately, Forgiveness is one of the most important factors in letting go. Regardless of the past hurt in your life, your journey to freedom will only begin when you forgive others.

I have heard countless people testify that when they release the spirit of resentment and forgave the person who hurt them, they experienced freedom. Choosing to forgive is making a deliberate choice to walk in peace. Hebrews 12:14-15 says, *"Pursue peace with all people and holiness, without which no one will see the Lord." Looking diligently lest any man fail of the grace of God: lest any root of bitterness springing up trouble you and thereby many be defiled."*

In fact, it is possible to experience God's peace in your life.

An important thing to note is that anyone who does not pursue peace by releasing offenses will eventually become defiled. I have personally made the choice to pursue peace, by releasing ill feelings and offenses. Pat Layton, in her book *"Life Unstuck",* suggested that "Freedom comes from surrender when we give our pain to God, He sets us free". In my opinion, letting go of the past, is not so popular, but one thing for sure, it is possible through the Power of God. Unforgiveness is a serious prison. It robs you of your joy, peace and contentment in serving the Lord. A person who harbours unforgiveness always loses out in life and is held hostage. In Mark 11:26, Jesus made it very clear that if you do not forgive then you will not be forgiven. You should forgive because it is also a command of God. *"And when ye stand praying, forgive, if ye have ought against any: that your Father also which is in heaven may forgive you your trespasses."* A person who cannot forgive has forgotten the great debt for which they were forgiven. However, it is clear to me that many excuses are given for harbouring unforgiveness and letting go. But if you practice being unforgiving you will not inherit the kingdom of God along with those who practice others sin.

PRACTICING FORGIVENESS

To become a better person, you must practice forgiveness. Failing to release past hurts will give the devil an opportunity to get a foothold in your life. In fact, you need to be on guard in your life so you will not allow the devil to gain entry through unforgiveness. Always be alert that the enemy is on the prowl, seeking to devour you .1 Peter 5:8 exhorts us: *"Be sober, be vigilant; because your adversary the devil, as a roaring lion, walketh about, seeking whom he may devour."*

Forgiveness offers total freedom and peace of mind. It is imperative that you let go of the unresolved hurts, pain or whatever ill circumstances and receive that complete release.

An incident occurred in my life as a teenager, involving a close family friend. On this particular day the person came to visit my home, while they were speaking to my mother I happened to walk nearby and went into the kitchen to finish cooking. To my surprise I heard the person speak to me in a loud critical tone saying, "but you can't cook? Is that the way you cook?' I was shocked at that blatant comment. The fact that I was taught growing up that you should not argue with adults but show them respect, at that very minute it was like a moment of laughter as my mother spoke out in my defense, yes man "she can cook" But the truth is I suppressed those thoughts of being hurt and put on a strong front when in reality I was deeply offended.

Even many months after the incident happened, whenever I saw the person, I could still feel the hurt lingering. I felt so withdrawn, in fact it was the torment from the unforgiveness. Yes, it is real! Unforgiveness holds you captive in the past. It is heavy and makes you feel burdensome and not wanting to let go. As a young Christian at the time, I remembered one day, while I was praying, I felt the Holy Spirit moving upon my heart, bringing to the light that matter that I needed to let go. Now it was time for me to let go of the unforgiveness! Instantly I began to replay the past hurt in mind and I could feel the emotions coming into the present. Letting go may not be easy but IT IS POSSIBLE!!! The truth is you can relive a hurt in your mind and feel it today just as vividly as when it happened twenty years ago.

Thank you, Lord, that even though I was stubborn in letting go, you reminded me of Your love and forgiveness, with tears running down my face. I am grateful for your grace and help in a time of need (Hebrew 4:16). The first step to freedom is to recognize you are hurt. Oftentimes, pride does not want you to admit you are hurt or offended. We must consider that pretending and covering up will keep you trapped and prevent you from being liberated. The moment I admitted to the true condition of my heart and was ready to embark on my journey of freedom, I could feel the difference. Thank you, Lord!!

No one can do it for you, you have to release the hurt and the pain. It is time to let go, leave the past behind. You must forgive the people who hurt you, as you journey through life. I have done that and will continue to practice forgiveness. Remember that the bottom line is the love of God. Glory to God! According to 1 Corinthians 13:5, *"love never fails, does not seek its own, it is not easily offended."* Letting go of the past is the right thing to do and you should not allow unforgiveness to block you from attaining Victory in your life. The Apostle Paul states in Philippians 3:13b that you must let go all that is behind you… *"But this one thing I do, forgetting those things which are behind, and reaching forth unto those things which are before."*

Looking at the life of Joseph in the book of Genesis, you will see that he had to forgive Potiphar's wife in order to go to his next level. Yes, Joseph had to let go the past hurt. No matter what you may have gone through in your life, today is your day of letting go.

In contrast, there are so many barriers in your past, but you can break free from them. This book *Moved to a New Mindset* that is now in your hands, has become a reality because I choose to LET GO OF THE PAST. Each day I made a choice to speak victory as I greet others. If you know me, I sure have a Victory Good morning hello for you. However, a new mindset means that you will have to be deliberate in choosing to live in victory, and that includes speaking it. As you are being renewed in your mind, hold this truth that you have to let go of the victim mentality.

YOU DO NOT HAVE TO BE A PRISONER OF YOUR OWN MIND

Life has so many challenges to offer, but you do not have to miss out on what God has in store for you by being a prisoner in your mind. Mental prisons are often built through fear, doubt or lack of confidence. It can grip you to the point that you, of yourself, are not even sure what it is that is holding you back. However, to break free from your mind prison, only depends on you. How many times have you thought that you will not be able to achieve something? Maybe because you may have seen someone else fail at doing it? At no time in your life, you should be looking at what others are achieving or not achieving. Here lies an important revelation that you need to grasp, learn to run your own race and stay in your lane.

Reflecting on what the scripture says in Philippians 4:13, *"I can do all things through Christ who strengthens me."* This has brought great hope to light that it is always possible to break out of the prison of your mind, yes you can escape mind prison. As you read this book, may the Spirit of the Lord remind you of any prison you are in and may you surrender to His bidding to walk free,

THE DOORS OF YOUR MIND PRISON ARE NOW OPENED!

The journey of freedom always begins in your mind. I concur with author Leostone Morrison, *"The poverty of a man resides not entirely upon the lack of economic possibilities but heavily upon the health and wealth of his mind."* No matter how unfair life seems or even if you have failed many times in the past, you can still win today by pursuing a renewed mind. All battles begin in the mind, and we can overcome the war in our Minds. In fact, it is one of the most valuable assets that God has given you.

Yes, you can experience mind renewal. Minds are still being renewed today. By the power of God embrace the wealth of the scripture as stated in Romans 12:2a. *"And be not conformed to this world but be ye transformed by the renewing of your mind..."*

SEE THE HAND OF GOD IN THE TRANSITION PHASE

My breakthrough lights are on, and I am seeing much clearer now what the Lord is doing and what He is about to do. Thankfully, the season I am in today is very important to me, because I am now able to make my future a great reality.

Life's journey sometimes brings great unpleasant events; but we can make it through with God's help. According to Philippians 1:6 *"God will complete anything he has begun in you".*

I am enthusiastic about the Lord's marvellous doing in my life. (Psalms 118:23)

In this transition phase of my life, I am seeing the hand of the Lord. I refuse to stay in limitations, doubt, and fear in the mind. Glory to God! I am in tune with the Lord calling me forth to the greater that He has in store for me. I have gotten the courage to move by faith.

37

It is a thrill to note that God is maximizing and bringing me into full potential of living on purpose. Restoration of the Breach School has taught me that mind renewal can push me to expand my thoughts beyond the regular. At one point, I entertained relationships with limitations. However, I soon realized that if I wanted to fulfil purpose, I would have to change my mindset. Having purposely divorced limitations I now understand what it means to be renewed in the spirit of the mind. (Ephesians 4:23)

You can never achieve what your mind has not perceived. Look what fear and limitations have done to me, they have caused me to create my own mind prison, and also operate from the low grounds instead of stepping out into Bold Exploits.

As I begin to dig deeper into God's Word and understand my purpose, I see the hand of God in the transition phase. God is at work in my life, and He has provided destiny helpers to walk with me in the process. Glory to God! I am acknowledging the Lord as He directs my paths (Proverbs 3:6). Then in Proverbs 16:3 He gave me more insight that He will establish by thoughts if I commit my works unto Him.

NEW MINDSET KEY

You are who your mind allows you to be. This is so true because every idea comes from a thought, whether great or not, it really begins in your mind. Whatever you may face in life, it is important to note that if you have doubted in your mind, you are already defeated.

The moment you think you do not have any money, that mindset of lack will invade your mind. However, if you embrace thoughts that God will provide the finances, instantly with that mind being renewed faith, the mountain of lack will be demolished.

Think about it! Once you think you can achieve something it is POSSIBLE to achieve it.

It is all in the state of the mind. Wow! This is just so powerful.

Once your mind allows you to believe that nothing is impossible, then your actions will be limitless regardless of your physical limitations. You become what you create in your mind. As your mind is renewed you find value not in being perfect but in purpose.

Here is a poem I learnt in Primary School:

All in the state of the mind- Walter D. Wintle

"If you think you are beaten, you are.
If you think you dare not, you don't.
If you like to win, but you think you can't,
It is almost certain you won't.
If you think you'll lose, you're lost
For out of the world we find, success begins with
a fellow's will. It's all in the state of mind.

If you think you are outclassed, you are, you've got to think high to rise, and you've got to be sure of yourself before you can ever win a prize.

Life's battles don't always go to the stronger or faster man, but soon or late the man who wins is the man who thinks he can!"

Proverbs 23:7:

"For as he thinketh in his heart, so is he: Eat and drink,

saith he to thee; but his heart is not with thee.

CHAPTER 3

THE COURAGE TO MOVE

Matthew 14:28-31

"And Peter answered him and said, Lord, if it be thou, bid me come unto thee on the water. And he said, Come. And when Peter was come down out of the ship, he walked on the water, to go to Jesus. But when he saw the wind boisterous, he was afraid; and beginning to sink, he cried, saying, Lord, save me. And immediately Jesus stretched forth his hand, and caught him, and said unto him, O thou of little faith, wherefore didst thou doubt?"

When God has a plan for your life, He has a way of bringing it to pass. Sometimes you may not understand His methods, but He always knows how to get it done. The fact that we may be in one place, God wants us to get the courage to move; but it takes faith. Jesus needed

Simon to move, He needed to see Simon stepping out in faith and trusting Him wholeheartedly.

Jesus wants you to step out of the boat, letting go of fears, doubts and limitations. It is natural that you see all different times of distractions when you are in a boat-like experience. Certainly, thoughts of feeling safe and secure will come, but today it is time to move out of that position. As you move in faith you are getting ready for the extraordinary that God has in store for you.

I am talking about the kind of courage where God asks you to step out of your comfort zone and walk on water with Him. I had to step out on water when I decided to trust God for the financial breakthrough to pay my son's college tuition. The truth is, I had no idea where the funds were coming from, but the moment I stepped out in faith, believe me, the application form was fully completed, and submitted. God came through with more than half of the school fee.

43

Glory to God! It is really rewarding to experience God's hand of provision. Looking back at that victory, I realize that trusting God will give you courage to move. Our God is not a God of limits; He makes it possible for you to keep moving forward even when you do not have the strength.

I can tell you it is easy to stand in the shallow waters because there are no challenges to be experienced. You are not tested; it is just comfortable and may be easy to run back to shore if things get difficult.

What I want to make clear is that after you have stepped out, you may still experience distractions and discouragement but with the power of a renewed mind you can beat all odds. What the Word of God says about you will always give you courage to move. You are exhorted with words of Philippians 1:6 that states; *"Being confident of this very thing, that he which hath begun a good work in you will perform it until the day of Jesus Christ"*. I thank God for the nudge in my heart, concerning the Mind Renewal Course, I wrestled with the thoughts, whether I should enrol or not. I eventually enrolled and I must say it was not easy leaving my comfort zone. I realized that I did not need strength to move forward, beyond my mind barriers. I needed courage. I thank God I made that intentional move.

KEEPING OUR EYES ON JESUS IS KEY

When Peter stepped out of the boat to walk to Jesus, he stayed afloat if he kept his eyes on Jesus. The moment he took his eyes off Jesus and put them onto his present situation, his faith faltered, and he began to sink.

How often do you get the courage to move forward and then, as you experience difficulty, you begin to sink? The reason for this is because you took your eyes off Jesus and began to look at the circumstances around you. There are so many areas of bondages that will make you hostage and prevent you from making that one move.

One such bondage is fear. Fear is a deep spirit that grips, and it is not from God. According to 2 Timothy 1:7 *"For the Lord has not given us the spirit of fear but of power, love and of a sound mind"*. To activate the courage to move will only be achieved by faith. The Bible did not leave you empty regarding faith. In 2 Corinthians 5:7, you see the following, *"For we walk by faith and not by sight"*. God does not want us to be ruled by fear that is why he gives us faith. If you are filled with unbelief and fear you will not be able to move. The truth is that the enemy will attack you by manipulating your thoughts. This is what God wills for us. In 1 John 5; 4 the scripture tells you; *"For whatsoever is born of God overcometh the world, and this is the victory that overcometh the world, even our faith"*. It is just so awesome to know that faith gives victory over worry and fear.

LIVING IN THE PRESENT AND THE FUTURE

Can you prepare for the future and accomplish goals without the courage to move? The thought of lost opportunities has made many people regretful for the rest of their lives. None of us embrace regrets; our desire should be to live on purpose and maximise our full potential. Yet we settle for less than the best life to live. Accepting limitations and doubts has robbed us of our great future. Do you want to experience a bright future? Then you must embrace that courage to move. It is time for us to take charge of our destiny and accomplish God's best in our lives.

It is very important to note that preparing for the future begins with the perceptions of the mind. We can never achieve our purpose or highest dreams if our minds have not perceived it. I must admit that it takes great courage to be completely honest with ourselves about what is keeping us stuck. It took courage for me to accept that I was stuck in limitations, rejections, and fears. The journey of freeing the mind must begin now; knowing that great things can be accomplished in your life. With this freedom you must maximize potential, and opportunities presented to you. However, it is time to step out of your mind and achieve your goals. I have made this bold step of faith; it was not easy at all. There are so many distractions around to cause you to take your eyes off Jesus. I know for sure that Jesus held my hand and I know He was so close to me; I just looked into His eyes and kept my mind stayed on Him. Isaiah 26:3 declares, *"Thou will keep him in perfect peace whose mind is stayed on Him"*. As you pursue Moving to a new mindset, just keep your eyes on Jesus.

The sky is the limit is a very powerful statement used to say that there is no limitation on what we can achieve in life and that anything is possible.

Yes, indeed!! You can achieve anything if you really want to, if you have the courage to move by faith. I recall singing this song in Sunday school:

> "I am a promise, I am a possibility, I am a promise, with a capital P. I am a great big bundle of potentiality, oh yeah. And I am learning to hear God's voice and I am trying to make the right choice; I am a promise to be anything He wants me to be"

It is so painful to see yourself settle for less in life, it is time to throw off the limits, and it is time to soar. Limitations are out of fashion; I have made a choice to stop wearing those outfits. There is so much better in store for you. Instead of being fully alive to the possibilities of the future that God has for you, you resigned yourself to existence without a vision. It is never too late to be great and to experience God's overflow. Now is the time to move, can I say that a little louder? NOW IS THE TIME TO MOVE!!!

Your circumstances may not look right, and the challenges you face may well be compared with that of Moses and the Israelites by the Red Sea. They were pursued by the Egyptians and Pharaoh's horsemen as stated in Exodus chapter 14. I challenge you to hold on to your faith, God is able and faithful to make the way in the midst of any difficulty. Always remember that your circumstances are ideal for the supernatural intervention of God.

It is very clear to me that not everyone has the same vision and perspective on things in life. I will certainly be pursuing whatever God has in store for me. It is such a vast domain; Jeremiah 29:11 is a verse you can cling to. It is a promise that reaches out to you with boundless hope *"For I know the plans that I have for you"* declares the

Lord", so when we accept the courage to move, He will give you an expected end.

SPEAK TO YOUR MIND

There is a tremendous battle going on in the mind at this point. However, it is very important that you speak to your mind by using the Word of God. You must boldly declare the Word of truth. Notice how the Psalmist declared, *"I shall not die but live and declare the works of the Lord". (Psalms 118:17)* In fact the moment you open your mouth and start declaring the Word, you begin to call to attention every fibre of your being that you will live. It does not matter how you may feel in your body right now. Just begin to speak to your mind; all ill health must go in Jesus' name. As a believer, begin to speak your mind, and you will receive the courage to make that move of faith.

51

The enemy may bring thoughts and suggestions to cause you to divert from believing what the Word of God says about your health, but now is the time to act against him and speak your mind. If you believe and speak the scriptures you are able to cramp and paralyze the enemy's schemes and tactics. Do you know that the Word of God always gives courage to move? I remember the scripture passage in Luke 5 when Jesus spoke to the fishermen who were trying to catch fish all night, but they caught nothing.

The scripture states in Luke 5: 4-5 *"Now when he had left speaking, he said unto Simon, launch out into the deep, and let down your nets for a draught"*. *"And Simon answering said unto him, Master, we have toiled all the night, and have taken nothing: nevertheless, at thy word I will let down the net"*

I am grateful that the Word is here to tell you, "It is time to let down your net. It is time to take courage and move. Too long, you may have been

52

in this position. It could be months, years, however in the case of the disciples it was all night long toiling. I am sure that thoughts of doubts may have come to their mind, pressing them to give up. At this time, it was a nevertheless moment for them. Look at the victory that came when they moved in faith. Let me tell you this, God has an abundant net breaking blessing awaiting you.

Speak to your mind and believe that your moment can be right now. You do not have to waver in uncertainty any longer. As your mind is being renewed you can grab on to this truth and move forward. It is time to take courage and move.

KEY POINTS – THE COURAGE TO MOVE

1. EVERYONE HAS A DIFFERENT PERSPECTIVE OF LIFE.

Persons have different goals and aspirations, which is dependent on their personal world- view and ideologies. In fact, some people are limited in their belief system and not wanting to move from where they are.

2. WE MUST BE INTENTIONAL IN MOVING FORWARD.

Now is not the time to be complacent and have a parked spirit about your life. You have to be intentional in pursuing moving to a new mindset.

It is time to get active in reading, studying and meditating on God's Word. When you allow the Word of God to transform you, it will give you power to reject doubts and limits in the mind systems. It is time to make that move of faith, according to Romans 12:2a *"And be not conformed to this world: but be ye transformed by the renewing of your mind…*You and I have to be intentional and take up the mandate of our own Mind Renewal.

3. TO REAP TOMORROW, YOU MUST MOVE NOW.

We are coexisting in the present and the future. - Leostone Morrison

Instead of moving forward there is a natural tendency in many of you to be passive in your lives. Let us go for it! Whatever you want to achieve begins now, not tomorrow. Now is the time to move in the mind. It is called Mind Renewal; that is the only way you can accomplish what God has in store for you. NO TO LIMITATIONS, NO TO FEAR. YES, TO THE WEALTH OF YOUR MIND!

4. MOVE FORWARD WITH RIGHT THINKING.

Whatever thoughts you engage in your mind is certainly what you will reap. So, begin to entertain good thoughts; it will pay big. How you invest in your mind will tell later. I am convinced that the secret to unlock the wealth of the mind is to be intentional in thinking about things that are right according to the scriptures. Hear what the word of God says in Philippians 4:8: *"Finally, brethren, whatsoever things are true, whatsoever things are honest, whatsoever things are just, whatsoever things are pure, whatsoever things are lovely, whatsoever things are of good report; if there be any virtue, and if there be any praise, think on these things".*

Often times the enemy may shoot thoughts to your mind that may seem desirable when they are really detrimental, but you have power through the scriptures. 2 Corinthians 10:5 reads, *"Casting down imaginations, and every high thing that exalteth itself against the knowledge of God, and bringing into captivity every thought to the obedience of Christ;"*

Spending time in God's Word always brings fruitful results in the life of the believer. Abiding in God's Word will bring wisdom.

DIFFERENTIATING BETWEEN SIGHT AND VISION

As I begin to explore the text *"Mind Renewal"*, written by Rev Leostone Morrison, I am beginning to connect more deeply with my purpose for doing the course. One thing for sure, I am not on this renewal Journey alone. The Holy Spirit is partnering with me and to bring it to completion. In Psalms 126:3, we read; ***"The Lord has done great things for me, and I am so glad".*** I am not walking by sight. As I continue the journey of my life, however, I have learnt that there are new territories to discover. Sight is the ability to see things as they are, while vision is the ability to see things as they could or should be. Rather than be confined to your current environment, vision sees beyond your now to

57

your future possibilities. The truth is that your vision is Mighty. Vision really reveals three dimensions, past present and future. It is critical that as you pursue the future, you always remember where you are coming from. It is very clear to me that the experiences in my past and knowledge of my present are coordinated into future plans and chartered courses. Bear in mind, that as long as you have a vision your future will be productive. The Bible declares in Proverbs 29:18; *"Where there is no vision, the people perish: but he that keepeth the law, happy is he."*

MOVING OUT

When I think about my previous position, being stuck in one place, and not making any move. It is a hard reality that one may be living their life and not maximizing their full potential. I can tell you; I know first-hand what that is like. When I think about my former posture it was filled with fear, limitations, doubt and anxiety, it felt like a handcuff that caused me not to move. In fact, even though you are yearning to make a move, it is not that simple. In the same matter, you cannot open the door of your house without a key, the same principle is applied if you have the courage to move. Thankfully God has provided the key of renewing the mind, and with that you can walk by faith, hand in hand with God to fulfill your divine purpose. Glory to God! Today when I reflect on where I was compared with today, the contrast seems incredible. Seriously, the time came for me to move out. The truth is, for a very long time, I was hanging out on limitations road. To be honest, that was one of my favorite places. I just never wanted to move too far. I just wanted to stay behind the scenes, but God had something much bigger in mind. Thank you, Lord! Today, I am walking boldly in faith and doing great exploits. In the past I feared what people would think of me, but now I am confident and feeling assured that I can do all things with the strength of the Lord (Philippians 4:13). I am no longer a victim of an impoverished mindset, but today I am walking in victory. I am no longer stuck, I have moved out, and I am now living in a wealthy mind.

It is my prayer that this book will inspire you to believe in God to take that courage to *Move To A New Mindset*. Nothing is impossible for Him. You can make any move as long as you are yoked to Him.

CHAPTER 4

STAND ON GOD'S WORD

As you begin to live your life from a renewed mind prospective, you will see that it is imperative that you stand on God's unfailing Word. Whatever God has said in His word; He cannot go back on it. In fact, the only way you can stand on the Word of God is to believe His Word and hold on to it. God makes eternal promises, and there is nothing more profound than the promises of a God who never lies. You can trust every word that He has spoken. You can have absolute confidence in God's reliability to make good on his promise because of his unchanging character. According to Hebrews 6:18 it is impossible for God to lie. Because he is a God of truth you can rest assured that He is a God of integrity. It is the integrity of God's character that makes it impossible for him to lie. In addition, the promises of God are established; He honours his word above his name. (Psalms 138:2) Today I am glad that I have access to His Word, and I can claim those promises. Do you know that the promises of God are His spoken word that is fully loaded to manifest in your life? Once God says something, it is already settled, and you must partner with the promise. The Word of God must not be slighted or doubted in any way. You can bank on the promises of God. God has already fulfilled many of the promises He has made to mankind in the past. God promised Abraham that through his seed all nations of the earth would be blessed (Genesis 22:18).

No matter how a situation looks in your life right now, you can stand on the sure promises of God. Growing up, I remember one of the hymns in our Redemption Songs book that was sung in our church services, *"Standing on the Promises of God."* The fourth verse reads, *"Standing on the promises I cannot fail."* This verse expresses a powerful truth: when standing on the promises of God, we cannot fall because the promises of God cannot fail. The Word of God is the only true foundation that you can stand on today, it is guaranteed to bring victory in your life and circumstances. Matthew 24:35 declares *"Heaven and earth shall pass away but my word shall not pass away"*. What a solid assurance! As long as you show up in faith, you will experience great wealth through the word of God as seen in John 14:14 *"If ye ask anything in my name I will do it"*. Today, you can start believing God for whatever He says He will do. **It does not matter what** is being presented in your difficult seasons, just stay your course having confidence that the promises of God are alive and waiting to be fulfilled in your life. You are also reminded to hold fast the profession of your faith without wavering as seen in Hebrews 10:23.

Through this Mind Renewal journey, I understand that God's Word is my only hope in the between period, you may ask what is the between? The between is that period linking the promise and the manifestation of God's Word. Not all the promises of God will come with pleasantries, you must go through the process, and it is very critical that you trust the Word of God. I can attest to this truth: that reading and studying His Word is crucial to our spiritual strength. There is a tremendous amount of peace through knowing and memorizing the scripture. On many occasions that I have faced difficulties, the Holy Spirit was on time to quicken a verse of scripture to my mind, or just to reassure me of his unconditional love.

According to Hebrews 4:12, the scripture reads, *"For the word of God is quick, and powerful, and sharper than any two-edged sword, piercing even to the dividing asunder of soul and spirit, and of the*

64

joints and marrow, and is a discerner of the thoughts and intents of the heart".

God's Word divides the soul and the spirit, and it is the only source that can renew your mind. Mind renewal is a process, and it does not come overnight. You have to be intentional about it. If you are going to give God a few minutes in a week, your mind will not be renewed.

The Word will not be implanted in you when you hurriedly read it. Oftentimes, you may know the scriptures with your head, but it is the engrafted Word in your spirit that changes you. Do you want to stand on the Promises of God? Then take the time to feed on the Word so you can be *rooted and built up in the faith. (Colossians 2:7)* When the Word of God controls your thinking it transforms your life.

THE PROMISES OF GOD BRING IMPACT!

"So shall my word be that goeth forth out of my mouth: it shall not return unto me void, but it shall accomplish that which I please, and it shall prosper in the thing whereto I sent it." Isaiah 55:11

Every word that proceeds out of the mouth of God has a powerful impact. His Word will not return unto Him void. It will accomplish what he has intended it to accomplish. God's Word has the power to set the course for change in your life. It is so powerful that it can break down barriers in the mind and give you a new mindset. Glory to God! The Word has done great things in my life, and I am so glad, (Psalms 126:3). The more I fill my mind with His powerful life-giving Word, and apply it to my life, the more I experience changes. I love the Word of God, and I am excited about sharing scripture verses with others. It is such a blessing to read God's Word. (Revelation 1:3) I am pursuing moving to a new mindset, so let me encourage you to take the time to get in the Word of God, read it daily, it is food to eat, that is what 1 Peter 2:2 tells us *"As newborn babes, desire the sincere milk of the Word, that ye may grow thereby"*. Study God's Word is a clear instruction as seen in 2 Timothy 2:15, *"Study to shew thyself approved unto God a workman that needed not to be ashamed, rightly dividing the Word of truth!"*. Meditate on it and let it change you from inside out. Joshua 1:8 gives us the remedy for meditating on the scriptures, *"This book of the law shall not depart out of thy mouth; but thou shalt meditate therein day and night, that thou mayest observe to do according to all that is written therein: for then thou shalt make thy way prosperous, and then thou shalt have good success"*.

"Draw nigh to God, and He will draw nigh to you"
(James 4:8)

The Spirit gives life; the flesh counts for nothing. The words I have spoken to you --they are full of the Spirit and life.

John 6:63. **This scripture has deeply ministered to my inner man.**

The Spirit is the one that gives life, human efforts accomplish nothing, and it offers no benefit at all. The Word is life; hence, Spirit and Life have resonated in my spirit and caused me to reflect on the fact that it is the Spirit of God that quickens sinners in such a manner that we are able to live. I am alive today because of the Spirit of God. What an amazing victory through the Word of God!

BELIEVE GOD'S WORD AND SPEAK IT!!

One of the weapons the enemy uses against you is doubt in your mind. The enemy will always try to hinder you from believing and receiving God's promises by faith. *"The Word of God is loaded with*

Power and is alive and active". (Hebrews 4:12) For you to allow the Word of God to explode in your life, start believing what it says about you and begin to speak it boldly. Many of God's people, regardless of how long they have been walking with Christ, need to believe and speak the Word of God. There is power in believing and speaking the Word of God. According to the scripture in *2 Corinthians 4:13: "I believed, and therefore have I spoken; we also believe and therefore speak".* Wow! It is so amazing that when you believe God's word for what it is and speak it over your own life, family and friends, God's explosive power is released and made manifest.

A few months ago, I had the privilege of sharing with some students about faith. Reading the scripture passage in Mark 11:23-24, *"Have faith in God. For verily I say unto you, that whosoever shall say unto this mountain, be thou removed, and be thou cast into the sea; and shall not doubt in his heart but shall believe that those things which he saith shall come to pass; he shall have whatsoever he saith".* As we went through the lesson, students expressed that they had not been delving into the power of speaking the Word, often. We examined the text and discovered that you must only have faith in God, believe in God's Word without doubting and speak what the scripture says about you. They were given a special assignment to declare the scripture out of their mouth. When they returned to class the following week, it was such a great joy to hear the students sharing that they were experiencing transformation in their thoughts, attitude and speech. Glory to God! This is exactly what God's Word has done to me, because it has creative power, it is impossible to be unfruitful. *"So shall my word be that goeth forth out of my mouth: it shall not return unto me void, but it shall accomplish that which I please, and it shall prosper in the thing whereto I sent it" Isaiah 55:11.*

The Word of God is now bearing fruit in every area of my life, marriage, and ministry. Whenever you discipline yourself to speak the Word of God. Watch out for the great harvest of blessings, victories, and favour. God's favour shoes look good on me, because I speak the Word of God. In this day and age with so many hardships and challenges, God intends for you to use *the Sword of the spirit which is the Word of God. (Ephesians 6:17)* You are in spiritual warfare and the enemy does not want you to be equipped for battle. The enemy may try to infiltrate your heart and sow seeds of doubt in your mind; but let me be clear about one thing: You can stand firm on God's Word. It is possible for you to declare it is written, just as how Jesus demonstrates to us in Matthew 4, how to handle the enemy even when he comes to tempt us: *"But he answered and said, "It is written, Man shall not live by bread alone, but by*

every word that proceedeth out of the mouth of God."
(Matthew4:4)

According to Proverbs 18:21, *"Death and life are in the power of the tongue"*. You have the power in your mouth to speak God's Words. So, whenever you begin to declare God's promises concerning your health you are establishing God's truth. You are tapping into the power of the Word by denying sickness the right to exist in your body. According to Galatians 3:13:

"Christ hath redeemed us from the curse of the law, being made a curse for us: for it is written, cursed is everyone that hangeth on a tree". Today you can take up your rightful position and speak God's Word. You have limitless power available to you. Yes, look at the ready missile right at your disposal to use against the spirit of infirmity. Let The Word of God explode in your life by speaking it today. You can choose to believe God's word in spite of what your circumstances look like. Do you want

some things to shift or change in your life? Then embark on this journey of renewing your mind.

PUT GOD' S WORD INTO PRACTICE

On the journey of renewing your mind, it is important that you put God's Word into action. Have you heard the expression, "practice what you preach?" In other words, instead of telling others to speak the Word, you must begin doing so by reading it often and be intentional about speaking it. Undoubtedly, the Word of God is so powerful that the more you practice speaking it, the frequency of it reflecting in your daily life will increase. Considering this, you must be mindful that whatever is not practiced will not be reflected in you. The key to practicing the Word of God is to be a doer of it. First, your attitude towards the Word of God is definitely a true reflection of your heart toward God Himself. The truth is that we give honour to God when we spend time in His Word. However, if you want to know how intimate you are with God, then begin to examine how much His Word means to you. Seriously, how much time do you give to the Word daily? Are you prioritising it or are you too busy for it? Now please understand that there is no way you can love God and not love His Word.

Today, you can make the commitment to be a doer of God's Word. It is never too late to begin. According to James 1:22 *"Be ye doers of the word and not hearers only deceiving your own selves"*. In fact, there are two types of persons shown here, the doers and the hearers. This is what the congregation in many churches look like today. The pastor will preach the Word, and many persons will hear it, but few will commit to do what it says.

It is your responsibility, in moving to a new mindset, to invite the power of God in your life so you can stand. However, to bask in the wealth afforded in this life, you need to be intentional about filling your mind with the Word of God and speaking it. The Word of God will then begin to *flow out of your belly like a well springing up into everlasting life (John 7:38)*

Your New Mindset awaits you!!

BE READY TO DECLARE THE WORD

Throughout the Bible, there are many powerful scriptures that you can declare over yourself, and you must practice declaring them boldly. God's Word is loaded with a wealthy supply of truth and power for every need. All you have to do is tap into your legal access in Jesus' name to faithfully declare God's Word in every situation that faces you. When a financial situation impacts you, speak the Word of promise that *God will supply that need. (Philippians 4:19)* When fear tries to take over, demolish it by speaking the Word. As 2 Timothy 1:7 states; *"the Lord has not given us the power of fear, but of power and love and a sound mind"*. Regardless of what happens, always hide the Word of God in your heart and speak it out. That is why it is important for you to be in God's Word every day, reading it, and meditating on the deep truths of the scripture.

You have to be intentional about hiding God's Word in your heart, that is what Psalms 119:11 states, *"Thy Word have I hid in my heart that I Might not sin against thee"*

The enemy may try to inflict you blow after blow, but I want to encourage you to lift up your shield of faith and speak God's Word. Whenever you lift your shield of faith you quench all the fiery darts of the devil. How many times have you remained silent and allowed the enemy to beat you up? Move to a new mindset is now the order of the day; you must dominate your thinking with God's Word so you can speak it. As you equip yourself with the ammunition of the Sword of the Spirit, you will be ready to hit back at the enemy when he strikes. Remember in John 4 when the devil came to tempt Jesus in the wilderness? Well, it was the weapon of the Word that Jesus used to counteract the enemy's plans, *"It is written"*. When your situation seems hopeless, you can draw for the Sword of the Spirit and use it against the devil. Make sure you always have your *"it is written"* ready and waiting to deal with the enemy. As your mind is renewed, always be ready to declare the Word of God. To speak the Word, it is key that you know the Word. How can we say we love God and not love His Word? A renewed mind results from diligently pursuing the knowledge of God.

In fact, true believers need to dominate their thinking with the infallible Word. It is time to get up and move into the kitchen of God's Word. Dish some food and eat your daily meal. The body of Christ has been infiltrated with the spirit of laziness and procrastination. It is time to take the Word of God more seriously, not as an on and off meal; but fervently seeking after God's Word. What a wealth to the mind, when you speak the Word.

In concluding this section, please allow me to say that I would be thrilled for the Lord to use these pages in any way possible to enhance your desire to speak the Word. Enforce victory in your life by what you say. As you faithfully speak God's Word, He will cause you to triumph. Glory to God! Look at the Power of God's Word Exploding in your life, when you begin to confess it. God is faithfully watching over His Word to perform it, fulfill it, and bring it to pass. (Jeremiah 1:12)

Our victory comes from the words we speak. When we speak the Word of God consistently, we will have the abundant life we want- so speak His Word faithfully.

"The tongue has the power of life and death, and those who love it will eat its fruit. Proverbs 18:21 (NIV)

SCRIPTURE PASSAGES TO DECLARE

* ❖ *Be ye doers of the word, and not hearers only deceiving your own selves. (James 1:22)*

* ❖ *I declare I am a doer of God's Word and not only a hearer. I am among those who hears the Word and do what it says.*

* ❖ *For we walk by faith and not sight. (2 Corinthians 5:7)*

* ❖ I declare that I am walking by faith and not sight.

* ❖ *For he hath made him to be sin for us, who knew no; that we might be made the righteousness of God in him. (2 Corinthians 5:21)*

* ❖ *I declare that I am the righteousness of God in Christ Jesus.*

* ❖ *I will praise thee; for I am fearfully and wonderfully made marvellous are thy works;*

and that my soul knoweth right well. (Psalms 139:14)

❖ *I declare that I am fearfully and wonderfully made by God.*

❖ *The righteous shall flourish like the palm tree: he shall grow like a cedar in Lebanon. (Psalms 92:12)*

❖ *I declare that I am flourishing like the palm tree.*

CHAPTER 5
EXPOSE YOUR SCARS

N o words could ever express how I felt when I had to open and share things about myself that I would not normally do. One thing I have to say is that you have to be honest and transparent enough, so you can help somebody else on their journey through life. Consequently, on the journey of the renewing of the Mind. You will have to come face to face with who you are as a person as well. I am convinced that Romans 8:28 is always at work: *And we know that all things work together for good to them that love God, to them who are the called according to his purpose*. God always works things out for our good and for his glory. Life is a journey that may have brought some challenges or obstacles in the various seasons. According to Merriam-Webster's Dictionary, the definition of a scar is a "mark left where something was previously attached" and "lasting moral or emotional injury" We all encounter some form of scars whether it be physical, emotional, mental or spiritual. However, you should not be ashamed of them but see them as your beauty scars that are unique to you. There is always a story behind a scar; however, many times people choose to hide or try to forget them. However, you should always expose them, they can become something beautiful if you use them to give God glory and help others. Great ministries can be birthed when scars are exposed. Despite what persons may have faced in their childhood, it has shown that someone going through the same situation or may have experienced something similar, is now encouraged and feels hopeful. As you move to a new mindset, be certain to grasp this concept: It is time to remove the mask and embrace those scars.

The Holy Spirit expressed Himself to me when he gave me the title of this book *Moved to a New Mindset,* in fact, you will have to make an intentional move in your mind so you can expose your scars. Some persons have worn masks for so many years that it is not easy for them to be themselves, for too long. The pain or hurt that they may have experienced is hiding behind a false impression of who they are, whether through self-confidence or spirituality. Outwardly, you praise and worship God as though you have never been wounded, much less scarred. However, the facade is to ultimately hide the truth of your pain from others and ourselves.

Unexposed scars are like termites eating away under the surface of our lives, now is the time to bring them to light so we can deal with them by the power of God's Word. Renewal of the Mind begins with embracing and accepting those scars. Whenever you cover the scars, you actually give the enemy weapons to use against you. It is like a secret bomb that the enemy has strapped to you which at any time can explode. Secrecy is one of the devil's tactics to destroy but we have received great wealth from the scripture that we are not *ignorant of the enemy's devices. (2 Corinthians 2:11)* Now is the time to march out and expose the scars, so you can receive your healing and move forward. This will definitely present you with a positive platform to motivate and propel ourselves to a higher place.

The unpleasant scenes of your life may have been vividly replayed in your mind, and it may seem like God, does not love you, but through those adversities come great success and victory.

The reality of these circumstances cannot be erased, but you can share the story. God is interested in healing your scars, so you will be able to speak about it without feeling pain. Your Scars will always allow you to be on a unique platform that gives God Glory. Great wealth and purpose are in scars; especially when we live a life that is pleasing to God. Others can come to know Christ through what we experienced.

We must make our scars the basis on which we are motivated to be a better person.

SCARS ARE REAL

Going through life with the burden of hidden scars can be extremely defeating. As our minds are renewed, we will stop being ashamed of our scars, and embrace them. A physical scar may leave a mark on your body, but it can be healed over time. Many persons will hide a scar that is on their body because they are ashamed of it or afraid of what others may say or think. But sharing is therapeutic. When you share your story, you receive healing and others are taught how to truly accept the God given beauty within. Some physical scars may take longer to heal than some but when they are healed, they will not hurt anymore.

The emotional scars in our lives are painful reminders that we have experienced hurts in the past and are still suffering from them. These types of scars speak to the ill treatment of one's emotions, leaving that person feeling fearful, guilty, and condemned. A few years ago, I was with my Church family on a beach trip. In close proximity to us there was a group of persons under a tree. While checking my lunch bag for food, I noticed a lady was sitting nearby on a tree stump with a baby in her arms. As I looked up in response to her movement towards me, she quickly seized the opportunity and started a conversation. I knew at once that the Holy Spirit was involved in this meeting. Her tone of voice was filled with disappointment and hurt. It was obvious that she had shared with others, her words began to overflow, not because I was listening, but she realized I showed empathy. She spoke of her childhood abuse, her history of broken relationships, and her despair for the future. The more she spoke, the more the tears ran uncontrollably down her face. It was obvious that she had experienced deep rejection, and a lot of emotional wounds. The Holy Spirit shifted my approach and guided me to talk about His love, and that God can move her beyond the pain and the scars into a meaningful purpose driven life. God can heal your scars so that you can be whole again.

It does not matter how old you are, and if your scars are not exposed and dealt with, a life filled without purpose will not reach its potential. Today you can choose to accept the beauty of the scars you carry by viewing them as God allowing them as a means of helping self and others.

In this day and age emotional scars will not be healed unless you become aware of how they are affecting you and then seek professional help. God is able to heal you and use you in spite of the emotional scars.

You must decide right now to push pass the disappointment, the rejection and touch God. Yes!!Your scars are beautiful tools; God can use them to develop great ministries, whether locally or internationally. "He gives us beauty for ashes".

You are extremely special to God, He calls you his peculiar treasure, and you are the apple of His eyes. Have you perceived who you are in Christ? The scripture calls you *"a chosen generation, a royal priesthood, a holy nation, a peculiar people; that ye should shew forth the praises of him who hath called you out of darkness into his marvellous light". (1 Peter 2:9)*

A personal encounter with God's Word in your life will give you the strength to move pass the wounded past and expose the scars in your life.

MOVED PASS THOSE SCARS

"And a certain woman, which had an issue of blood twelve years and had suffered many things of many physicians, and had spent all that she had, and was nothing bettered, but rather grew worse When she had heard of Jesus, came in the press behind, and touched his garment. For she said, if I may touch but his clothes, I shall be whole". (Mark 5:25-28)

In Mark Chapter 5, the scripture tells of a woman who had an issue for twelve years and she had to push passed many things to touch Jesus and receive her healing breakthrough.

She had been suffering from this bleeding condition for a long time, and it had caused her to feel drained and hopeless. Her situation had affected everything about her. She had spent all her money going to various doctors without much help. Her desperation was so overwhelming that she no longer cared what others thought. I believe this situation had scarred her for so long that she decided that the time had finally come for her to move pass those scars. At this point in her life, all that she wanted was to get her healing deliverance. Consequently, she had to make an intentional move to push through the crowd.

I can imagine that as she made her way to Jesus, perhaps the thoughts of the past were trying to invade her mind. Nevertheless, she pushed through the crowd, holding on to her Never-Give- up faith. This woman only wanted to touch Jesus' garment. I believe the thickness of the crowd caused her to move closer to Him. Letting go of emotional scars requires faith in God. There is no room for doubt and fear when you need a miracle. Move to a new mindset with this truth, *"Do not watch the crowd, make your way forward"*. *"And straightway the fountain of her blood was dried up; and she felt in her body that she was healed of that plague. And Jesus, immediately knowing in himself that virtue had gone out of him, turned him about in the press, and said, who touched my clothes? And his disciples said unto him, thou seest the multitude thronging thee, and sayest thou, who touched me? And he looked round about to see her that had done this thing but the woman fearing and trembling, knowing what was done in her, came and fell down before him, and told him all the truth. And he said unto her, Daughter, thy faith hath made thee whole; go in peace and be whole of thy plague". (Mark 5:29-34)*

The Bible says that the very moment she touched Jesus, immediately the issue that had plagued her for twelve years dried up! Glory to God! Her touch was different from all of the others in the crowd, because it was a gentle touch of faith and God always responds to faith. You can receive complete healing and deliverance if you make a choice to move pass those scars. Your great physician is Jesus, and if you allow those past

91

wounds and scars to press you towards Him, you will receive your breakthrough

4 KEY POINTS ABOUT SCARS

1. Do not be ashamed of your scars, they always tell a story.
2. Scars are unique to each individual, so wear them well!!!
3. Everyone one has a story. It does not matter how scarred or bruised you are; God can use you big time.
4. God never wastes a hurt or a scar he has use for every one of them.

MY GREATEST SCAR: ON A PERSONAL NOTE

Having learnt that I was not supposed to be born, I became scarred with rejection from a young age. My parents had seven children already and there were absolutely no plans for another child. The truth is, that my mother, who had a wealthy mind, decided that she would not give up purpose. When she separated from my father and his abuse, she took me with her at four years old. Subsequently, I never grew up with my siblings, however, our relationship has been one of great togetherness. I have come to realize that once God has a plan for your life, even before you were born, there will be a battle against that purpose. Jesus has already prepared a way; He is the way.

Sometimes, having thoughts of feeling rejected would surface and I felt depressed and withdrawn; but today I am embracing and exposing the scar of rejection. I am filled with God's Purpose!

"Rejection is never always a bad thing"- Rev. Leostone Morrison

"Look at the Lord's doing, it is indeed marvellous in our eyes". (Psalms 118:23)

I am a living testimony about God's divine plan for my life; it is just amazing what God has done for me.

The greatest investment in my life was when I accepted the Lord Jesus. Well, looking back now, I realize that when Jesus saved me, He brought comfort with the revelation that He loved and wanted me. Glory to God, He has helped me to get over the rejection I had felt, brought healing to my emotions, and renewed me. What a love is on display here!! He has brought me to an understanding of Jeremiah 29:11 which says, *"For I know the thoughts that I think toward you, says the Lord, thoughts of peace and not of evil, to give you a future and a hope"*. Wow! What a promise word! I think this verse expresses God's heart about me, and it just humbles my heart.

I am predestined to be here; I am called and set apart by my heavenly Father. The scripture that flows out of my heart is Psalms 139:14 and it reads, *"I will praise thee; for I am fearfully and wonderfully made: marvellous are thy works; and that my soul knoweth right well"*.

I am intentional about moving to a new mindset; Praise God the Holy Spirit has imparted wisdom for me to begin. He has saturated me with His Spirit, an overflow of God's power and purpose poured out from me to others. What a gift that is, recognizing my total dependence is on Christ. Doing the Scripture Drill Bible Programme that I currently do, I engage in studying the scriptures daily and the Lord has presented opportunities for me to teach others about this important discipline. You see, no matter the scar, Jesus is with you. It is now time to move to where God wants you to be. God bless you Reverend Morrison! I thank God for your obedience to move when God told you to begin the Restoration of the Breach School Without Borders, I would not have exposed this scar if it were not for this course. I am now free to give God my scar as I share its beauty and God's empowerment with others.

Can you imagine! God ministered marriage to my heart years ago, even though my parents separated and were never married. Certainly, with God, nothing is impossible. I could not envision the Ministry of Marriage Coming forth! Mighty God! What a journey!!! I am overwhelmingly and irreversible blessed by the Lord's doing in my life.

After all, as believers, you and I must understand we are on the verge of discovering a new momentum in our life. As you move to a mindset grasp this truth: You must equip yourself to be a better person. Getting knowledge, reading books, investing in others, and expanding your mind. My scars will certainly Give God Glory! I wear a smile that only God gave!!! I know it is beautiful!!

It is time to stop being ashamed of your scars, embrace and wear them proudly, because when you do that, they validate and express the real you. Yes, you can share your testimony and help someone along life's journey. Indeed, your scars make you beautiful. In John 10:10 Jesus said, *"The thief cometh not, but for to steal, and to kill, and to destroy: I am come that they might have life, and that they might have it more abundantly"*. The enemy comes to destroy, but God has given you abundant life, past hurts and scars are weapons the devil seek to use to rob you of your dreams and a bright future. Again, your scars make you beautiful.

Wow! That is powerful. You will find your purpose out of your pain, hurt, ridicule and indifference. Thank You Lord for teaching me how to move to a new mindset so that, through my scars, I now have a platform from which I can motivate others.

NOT ASHAMED OF SCARS -Minister Heath's Testimony

Jeremiah 32:27

"Behold, I am the LORD, the God of all flesh: is there anything too hard for me?

When I see transformation taking place in somebody's life, I say, "look what the Lord hath done"! While watching an interview with Minister Heath, I was blessed by his openness to share about himself. This Man of God was more than willing to expose the scar of illiteracy and the many challenges that he faced. He was not interested in covering up anything that happened in his life. He had a testimony, and he was ready to share it with the world. Today the scar of illiteracy has brought forth a platform where he is a motivational speaker and Gospel Artist. Glory to God! Minister Heath further exposed his incarceration which led to his personal encounter with God.

It is awesome and amazing to see God take someone out of the chaos that they have been living in and bring them into a place of graceful purpose. Being on death row was another part of his journey. He confidently declared that when the Lord has favoured you, no one can stop it! What a testimony of deliverance and victory. The Lord has favoured this man of God. As he journeyed through tests, trials, and life's sufferings at the end of the day, he was never ashamed of his scars. Additionally, so great was his confidence and enthusiasm that Minister Heath willingly shared his telephone number inviting anyone who believes God will fail, that they should give him a call.

His salvation experience gave him boldness to declare his involvement in the fellowship and the love for God. What a transformation in his life! Psalms 126:3 assures you that "*The Lord has done great things*".

TAKEAWAYS FROM EXPOSING YOUR SCARS

1. **We can live our resurrected life in Christ. No matter how dead things look, God can resurrect lives.**

2. God is able to drop charges. He can do exceedingly and abundantly; nothing is impossible with him. He can drop charges and gives us freedom in Christ.

3. A message of transformation is available through Christ. Only what Christ has done for us can bring transformation.

4. The Power of our scars awaits our activation. (4b) So Much Purpose is in your scars, they all await activation. (4c) Do not be afraid to step out and activate.

5. Do not be afraid to tell your story. Sharing what you have been through always helps someone else.

6. Do not give the devil ammunition by hiding your scars. The enemy's plan is to plague your mind with shame, guilt and condemnation but do not allow him to have any secrets for you.

7. You cannot talk about the mess until you have gotten over it. It is very important to confront so you can conquer.

8. Accept criticism and ridicule, they can unlock great possibilities in your life. Moving to a new mindset has brought new strength to the fore, no matter what people say about you, hold fast to who you are in God.

9. Irrespective of the limitations you have, God has a great purpose for your life.

10. If you do not have the resources, God can still make a way for you. Great Provider, Almighty God has always made the way when there seems to be no way. Lack of

resources is not a deterrent from going to school and excelling.

CHAPTER 6
IMPERFECT BUT VALUABLE

It is not by accident or pure coincidence that you are at this chapter. I think there is a phenomenal upgrade taking place in your mind that you continue to read this book. You will be able to see yourself as being valuable, despite the imperfections. There is no perfect person here, God is still working on us, He is chiselling away some stuff. My continuous journey through the Mind Renewal Course has caused me to see that my flaws, imperfections, and leaks were positioning me to do great exploits.

Through cracks or imperfections, you will see greatness; however, it is the flaws that make your life more meaningful. Indeed, you may have sustained injuries or a lot of blows as you go through the different seasons of life. Recognize that in spite of the blows of negative, judgmental

103

criticisms those were quite useful for God to carve out the vessel He is designing. Interestingly this battle is about your great purpose, vision, and destiny so you will come face to face with great obstacles. The enemy may seek to destroy you because he is on a mission to break you. However, *"No weapon formed against you shall prosper". (Isaiah 54:17)* Pay close attention here, the devil wants to devalue you in your thoughts about your worth. The Bible tells us in 1 Peter 5:8:

"Be sober, be vigilant; because your adversary the devil, as a roaring lion, walketh about, seeking whom he may devour".

Do not settle for the lies of the enemy. You are a masterpiece in God's hand. You may not even fully understand your value right now, but do not be perturbed. The truth is that God's Word has expressed this beautiful truth in Psalms 139:14; *"You are fearfully and wonderfully made."*

You may experience a few cracks and bruises, but you are still here. You are blessed by God to live. God specializes in imperfect vessels, and He is able to make valuable vessels out of them. God is committed to work on you. He will use His Word to correct, correct and comfort you. Wow! The best part is that God will make a complete work of art out of you. Philippians 1:6 *"being confident of this very thing, that He who has begun a good work in you will complete it until the day of Jesus Christ".*

"As you renew your mind, refrain from being consumed with what appears to be your shortcomings"- Leostone Morrison

No matter how marred, bruised or imperfect you may be right now, God who is the architect of your life can find great worth in you. Always remember that your uniqueness is embedded in your flaws, and they set the stage for you to be used powerfully. It is said in Psalms 100:3, *"It is He that has made us and not we ourselves".*

105

When someone is impacted by the challenges of life, they may become broken, but when they are able to go through and overcome through the strength of God, then a valuable vessel is created. Looking at how God uses broken vessels is just so amazing. He has a way of bringing great transformation to lives. God never throws away broken vessels. He has use for every one of them. When I think about a cracked pot, I see that it can be used to plant a beautiful flower, and then put it at the side of the fence. Today you may be cracked with flaws but guess what? God can use you to be a centrepiece on His dining table. You can never fathom how God works; He has great use for you.

You are valuable in the sight of the Lord. It is always a blessing to hear persons who have been bruised share their testimony, about the goodness of God in their lives. Even persons around them may have given up on them. But God never rejects anyone. He is the Master Potter, and He is still working on imperfect vessels, so He can make them valuable again. How many times have you seen people that are in awe or shock at the Lord's doing? God is still in the business of blowing minds with uncommon victories, favors, restoration, and renewal in person's lives. Undoubtedly God, who is a God of love, will always use brokenness or flaws to create something great.

The Apostle Paul was on a path to destroy the Christians, but when he got that encounter on Damascus Road, we see how God used him greatly.

Philippians 1:6: "Being confident of this very thing, that he which hath begun a good work in you will perform it until the day of Jesus Christ".

I have seen the Lord perfect some things the enemy tried to use to buffet me, but God has always kept His hand on my life. Even though the imperfections and flaws seemed innumerable, I realize God used me, nonetheless. I am continually amazed how God uses me, just an ordinary person who is willing to be used for Christ's sake. Thank you, Lord, for revealing those treasures within me and letting me know that my flaws are of great value. The more you experience different circumstances in life, the affliction, the disappointment, hurts, and pain, bear in mind that God is preparing you for something greater.

Have you ever felt that you were unqualified, imperfect, or inexperienced to be used by God to fulfil His purposes? Well, you are not alone, bear in mind that we are all imperfect, and we have *all fallen short of the glory of God. (Romans 3:23)*

As you lift your faith and trust God, believe His Word Philippians 4:13 says, *"I can do all things through Christ who gives you strength"*. It is guaranteed and established in the truth of the scripture that God can use you. I have seen it personally in ministry over and over where God uses persons that are broken, hurting, and wounded and they make a big difference in the Kingdom of God.

A woman that has experienced emotional wounds, was able to minister to hurting women and give them hope because of the transforming power of God in her life. Unfortunately, man sees you for who you are, but God sees you for who you can become. Many times, I am looked at as being imperfect because of my flaws, but God always uses my weakness to give Him glory. Thank you, Jesus!!

Consider what the scripture says in 1 Corinthians 1:26-29 *"Brothers and sisters, think of what you were when you were called. Not many of you were wise by human standards; not many were influential; not many were of noble birth. But God chose the foolish things of the world to shame the wise; God chose the weak things of the world to shame the strong. God chose the lowly things of this world and the despised things and the things that are not to nullify the things that are, so that no one may boast before Him". (NIV)*

We need to remember that in God's eyes everyone is of great value, and He also uses the foolish. Today I want to encourage you as you journey with me in my moved to a new mindset experience, that you begin to embrace your weakness so that the power of Christ can rest upon you and His greatness will be displayed in your life. The Apostle Paul tells us in 2 Corinthians 12:9; *"And he said unto me, "My grace is sufficient for thee: for my strength is made perfect in weakness. Most gladly therefore will I rather glory in my infirmities, that the power of Christ may rest upon me".*

Do not let the mistakes of the past keep you in mind prison, nor let your imperfections keep you from serving God. Do a victory dance, you are valuable in God's sight. Believe this truth, God is well able to use persons with flaws for His service, however, most of us would have never even considered them. I believe that God is unimpressed by eloquent speech and educational qualifications. He can use you to do great things, however, do not get me wrong here. Knowledge and skills may be good. In fact, if you lack wisdom, you should ask God for it (James 1:5) When it comes to God, it is a whole new perspective. Yes! You will begin to see yourself with a new purpose and of great value in your life.

In the Bible we see many characters who have imperfections, but God used them mightily. Let us look at three men who were used by God and see what we can learn from their lives.

PAUL'S IMPERFECTION

The Apostle Paul was on a path to destroy the Christians, but when he got that encounter on Damascus Road, we see how God used him greatly.

"And Saul yet breathing out threatenings and slaughter against the disciples of the Lord, went unto the high priest, and desired of him letters to Damascus to the synagogues, that if he found any of this way, whether they were men or women, he might bring them bound unto Jerusalem". (Acts 9:1-2)

He was definitely a chosen vessel, based on his conversion. God uses the unlikeliest of persons despite their imperfections.

"And as he journeyed, he came near Damascus: and suddenly there shined round about him a light from heaven: And he fell to the earth, and heard a voice saying unto him, Saul, Saul, why persecutest thou me? And he said, Who art thou, Lord? And the Lord said, I am Jesus whom thou persecutest: it is hard for thee to kick against the pricks. And he trembling and

astonished said, Lord, what wilt thou have me to do? And the Lord said unto him, Arise, and go into the city, and it shall be told thee what thou must do". (Acts 9: 3-6)

Looking at Paul's flaws, you can see that they were not a curse, but they were a blessing to keep him humble to perform. I will certainly not allow imperfections to hinder me; I will do what God bids me to do. My flaws, according to Jesus, are not a curse but a golden opportunity for the glory of God to be revealed. Yes! Lord manifest through my flaws!!! Your grace is sufficient for me, and my strength is made perfect in weakness. Paul was a bruised vessel but performed and gladly revealed his weakness, knowing God's strength is perfected in it. *"And he said unto me, my grace is sufficient for thee: for my strength is made perfect in weakness. Most gladly therefore will I rather glory in my infirmities, that the power of Christ may rest upon me". (2 Corinthians 12:9)*

113

We all have unique purposes and destinies to fulfil. At times you may perceive flaws as imperfections, when in fact they were meant to create something beautiful and unexpected. Therefore, it is very important to identify internal and external factors in ourselves because they help us to identify strengths and weaknesses in our personality that will help us to build a perception of ourselves.

DAVID'S IMPERFECTION

David is a good example. Some of his imperfections were adultery and other sins. But in Psalms 51: 7-12, he repented, and God was able to use him.

"Purge me with hyssop, and I shall be clean: wash me, and I shall be whiter than snow. Make me to hear joy and gladness; that the bones which thou hast broken may rejoice. Hide thy face from my sins and blot out all mine iniquities. Create in me a clean heart, O God;

and renew a right spirit within me. Cast me not away from thy presence; and take not thy holy spirit from me. Restore unto me the joy of thy salvation; and uphold me with thy free spirit".

As you examine this scripture in Psalms 51 you will see that if you repent there is still hope for you. You can experience a fresh start. David took responsibility for his actions and confessed his sin. The Lord being so gracious forgave him and released him from the adultery and murder. What a God of forgiveness! When you confess your sins; he forgives you beyond measure. According to Psalms 103:12 your sins are removed from you.

"As far as the east is from the west, so far hath he removed our transgressions from us." (Psalms 103:12)

From God's perspective, He has use for you.

Now is not the time to allow mind binding thoughts to grip you. If you are willing to allow

115

God to do the repair on any cracks, bruises or imperfections, you will share a testimony. He is a God of a second chance. God sees so much greatness in you and His word to you right now is …... YOU MAY BE IMPERFECT BUT YOU ARE VALUABLE!

MOSES IMPERFECTION

"And Moses said unto the LORD, O my LORD, I am not eloquent, neither heretofore, nor since thou hast spoken unto thy servant: but I am slow of speech, and of a slow tongue". (Exodus 4:10)

As you consider the life of Moses, you will see that he was imperfect. He had speech problems which resulted in him lacking confidence to speak. Therefore, he made several excuses not to serve God in his leadership position. How many times have you made excuses to avoid doing what God calls you to do? Moses, like many of us, was quick to question God, and asked the Lord "why me"? You may end up pointing out all your disabilities, flaws and all the reasons you are incapable of doing what God ordained you to do. It is all about the excuses right here.

God does not need your ability to do anything, all He needs is your availability and most importantly, your obedience. Once you are ready and willing to show up, He is willing to equip you and use you in His kingdom. I have seen God use Mighty men and women in the kingdom that he has equipped for leadership.

It is certainly not about educational qualifications when it comes to what God wants to do. You may be unqualified in the eyes of others, but God is always ready to use you. The very moment Moses surrendered to the call of God his journey began. In my first year of high school, I remember being told by my form teacher to prepare to read my essay in class. I believed just like Moses; I was quick to make excuses that I cannot speak in front of the class. One thing for sure, thoughts of doubts and fears were the first guests to visit my mind. I was so nervous and afraid that when I arrived home from school, I told my mother about it with deep fear gripping me. I thank God for a mother who never refused to listen, she took it seriously and offered words of affirmation that I can do it and I should remember to keep God's word in my heart (Philippians 4:13). There are so many valuable children walking around trapped in the fear of imperfections.

I believe that parents/guardians should support their children to help free them from their fears. With the encouragement that I got, I received strength and courage to step out and read in the class. It was not as difficult as I thought. See what I have been saying throughout this book, everything that you do begins in your mind. As you move to a new mindset grasp this truth: God can use you even when you do not believe He can.

KEY POINTS TO CONSIDER:

1. GOD CAN USE YOU IN SPITE OF YOUR IMPERFECTIONS.

With a renewed mind, you will be able to see your flaws and embrace them, knowing that there is purpose in your brokenness. Moses was used by God despite his stutter.

No matter what you have been through, God can use you.

2. GOD PAYS ATTENTION TO IMPERFECT VESSELS.

You are the clay and God is the Potter. There are times when you do not have a say in the matter.

The Lord knows how to fashion you and make you into the vessel he wants.

119

Fiery circumstances are not always bad; God can use them to make you into a better person.

3. REFRAIN FROM BEING CONSUMED WITH WHAT APPEARS TO BE YOUR SHORTCOMINGS.

Moving to a new mindset with God's Truth is an excellent path to ride over your imperfections."

These shortcomings can be used as self-confidence too. The shortcomings even make you standout and God is able to use you. Feeling guilty easily is one shortcoming I sometimes face. God has used this to allow me to truly care about the needs of other persons.

4. APPRECIATE OTHERS WITH THEIR IMPERFECTIONS AND FLAWS.

The wealth of one's mind is unshackled when they can appreciate others with their imperfections and flaws. Seeing others differently can only be perceived from a place of Mind

120

Renewal, accepting them, showing them empathy and love, and being more tolerant.

5. MOVE TO A NEW MINDSET BY SERVING NOT FOR PRAISES.

Refuse to harbour resentment and be bitter because people fail to appreciate the work you have done. Instead, serve for the joy of contributing.

WITHOUT LEGS BUT VALUABLE –The Story of Nick Vujicic

Move to a new mindset with this truth, everyone is here for a purpose. Each of us has something to give. As a matter of fact, If God can use Nick Vujicic, a man without arms, and legs then he can certainly use a willing heart. There are no limits in God. Vujicic began to accept his imperfection and work through it as he grew older. By the time he was a teenager, Vujicic had mastered doing nearly everything a non-disabled person can do.

121

When Nick was asked if he prayed to God for arms and legs, He said yes, every now and then. In fact, he was more focused on making impacts on persons' lives. You do not have to be consumed with flaws or disabilities. It is time to embrace who you are as your mind is renewed daily. Nick also said it is such a joy in such a unique and powerful way to create impacts. He has looked pass his limbs and his body to something more important, his spirit and attitude.

That is so awesome!!!

BELIEVE THAT YOU ARE VALUABLE

As you move to a new mindset, it is imperative to believe that you are valuable and that you are worthy to give of yourself. For you to know how valuable you are you must begin to accept God's unconditional love. The way God looks at you is through the lens of His love. In the thirteenth chapter of 1st Corinthians, you will see love being expressed and how God feels about you.

"Charity suffereth long, and is kind; charity envieth not; charity vaunted not itself, is not puffed up, Doth not behave itself unseemly, seeketh not her own, is not easily provoked, thinketh no evil; Rejoiceth not in iniquity, but rejoiceth in the truth; Beareth all things, believeth all things, hopeth all things, endureth all things. Charity never faileth: but whether there be prophecies, they shall fail; whether there be tongues, they shall cease; whether there be knowledge, it shall vanish away". (1 Corinthians 13:4-8)

Look at how love is expressed in the above scripture passage. First God wants you to see that because He loves you, He is patient with you in every aspect of your life. Glory to God! What love! As you become secure in God's love you will discover that you are indeed valuable.

If you are reading this book and you have not accepted Jesus Christ as your personal Saviour, consider doing so today. God wants to use you. Now is not the time to make excuses! Your flaws, and imperfections are just perfect for God to maximize in your life. *NO SITUATION IS BEYOND THE REACH OF GOD!* Nothing is too hard for Him. (Jeremiah 32:27) On some occasions it may feel as though God is not there or He has forgotten you. However, the truth is, that God loves you, unconditionally, He values you and wants to save you. (John 3:17) No matter how difficult and complicated your situation may be, God is able to turn things around. With God in the equation of your life, your future is guaranteed, and everything is subjected to change.

CHAPTER 7
EMBRACE THE BETTER ME

THERE IS MORE TO BE DISCOVERED AS YOU PURSUE A BETTER YOU.

Moving to a new mindset is imperative in the life of every believer. Looking where I am now, because of the grace of God. I realize that there is so much more about me that I need to discover. The better version of myself is not far-fetched, it is attainable with God. Certainly, the truth is expressed in Luke 1:37, *"With God, nothing is impossible"*. However, as you embark on life's journey, you will learn that there is a battle in who you are and who you are becoming. In fact, I strongly believe that the whole aspect of renewing the Mind should be introduced in early childhood days. My reason for saying this is that young children will learn that they can excel at whatever they do. They do not need to compare

125

with others but embrace the fact that it is possible to become a better version of themselves. Excellent thought patterns are in realizing who you can become. They have great impact on your development. The truth is, what you think about yourself is more important than what you do. Are you beginning to see the picture? To embrace the better you, it can only begin when you enter into a personal relationship with Christ. Too many persons want to be better, without having a relationship with Christ and that is just not possible. Of course, there is always a war that is going on in the mind that wants you to live a life of limits or on the contrary life that will pursue the better version of yourself.

The Apostle Paul describes this war in Romans 7:15 when he declared that *"For that which I do I allow not: for what I would that do I not: but what I hate, that do I"*.

126

Becoming a better person is a continuous process. Life is all about growth and development. In fact, God wants you to accomplish great things in your life, and for you to make a positive impact in this world. God did not create you with limitations on his mind. He wants us to live a life of full potential. He has placed many gifts, talents, and a wealth of potential within you and so you must keep growing and excelling because He has great things in store for you.

As you navigate the seasons of your life, you will encounter various challenges, experience many failures, and gain success along the way. Importantly, you will discover that even being intentional about the portions that you eat is a part of being a better person. Eating healthy always leads you to a healthier life. As I mentioned earlier in this book, you can accomplish what is conceived in your mind. A lot more will be revealed as you pursue the better

127

version of yourself. Rejecting the impoverished mindset and embracing a wealthy mind has brought a lot to my view as I seek to let the unique me be expressed. Owing to the Adamic nature, we have all sinned and fallen short of God's glory. Therefore, to become a better version of yourself, you must totally yield yourself to the Spirit of God. "Yes! You must be devoted and intentional about your commitment."

HOW TO BECOME A BETTER PERSON

Becoming a better me, I must be honest with myself about the positives and negatives.

However, being a prisoner of my mind has caused me to doubt, fear, procrastinate and avoid stepping out. In the past the spirit of fear had held me in a whole lot of shackles. Hostage in the mind is a real thing! Let me tell you about that. It is a dominant force that holds you in a place where you just cannot move. It is filled with droplets of procrastination for example, planning to improve yourself by going back to school and because of that handcuff of the mind, you just cannot move. As my mind is being renewed, I am better able to understand that I will improve even in the ministries that I serve, whenever the better me starts coming forth! I am now able to unlock the wealth of my mind, through the transforming Word of God, which is my benchmark. The more you embrace the Word of God, the greater your ability is to deal with persons who may have offended you. In 1 Peter 4, God made it clear about love *"And above all things have fervent charity among yourselves: for charity shall cover the multitude of sins". (1 Peter 4:8)*

Love is the Master key here, certainly you become a better person when you allow the fruit of the spirit to manifest in your life. Love really makes you stand out. Others will know that you are different because of the love of God. I would like to take a moment to reflect on my experience as a Christian- as a part of the bride of Christ. God's love is so great that he will extend his hand of forgiveness even when I have done wrong. Can you imagine the difference it makes when you extend His love to others? Wow! What a love here. So if you want to see the better you, BEGIN WITH LOVE! God's abundant love in your heart, shed abroad by the power of the Holy Ghost, has made it possible. The Bible speaks about this love in Romans 5:5 and it reads' *"And hope maketh not ashamed; because the love of God is shed abroad in our hearts by the Holy Ghost which is given unto us".*

Now is my time. I am embracing the better me, yes! Yes! Refocus, renewed mindset, breaking free from handcuffs of the mind, no longer being influenced by others' opinion, but influenced by the Power of the Word of God. Look and you will see that the "No limitation sign is up" I am not limited! Certainly, I am rejecting the low ground and stretching my mind to inhabit higher frequencies. My new song is "Bye. Bye, Goodbye to doubt and procrastination in Jesus' name. the same is available to you-move to a new mindset.

IN ORDER TO ACHIEVE A BETTER ME, I MUST CONQUER SOME THINGS AND REALIZE SOME DREAMS.

MY CONQUER LIST

- ❖ Take responsibility for myself
- ❖ Let go of the past
- ❖ Focus on my own path
- ❖ Always be grateful
- ❖ Do not chase money, but chase purpose
- ❖ Focus on now
- ❖ Give my all and be enthusiastic about what I do.
- ❖ Do not wear a mask in order to fit into the world.

131

- ❖ Never stop learning,
- ❖ Feed my mind with strength.
- ❖ Walk alone, if I have to.
- ❖ Continuously strive with integrity
- ❖ Break free from fear
- ❖ Keep on going & growing
- ❖ Fight for what I want
- ❖ Remembering it is never too late to be great.

Do not be derailed by jealous people

WORKING ON MYSELF

When I think about working on myself, my thoughts reflect on school days. In fact, I always remember those Mathematics tests results that brought some low grades and there I was thinking about doing better next time. That is how God wants us to pursue and become better versions of ourselves. I suggest that we should be intentional about getting things done, so we can improve ourselves. In this day and age of casual faith, too many persons have allowed themselves to slide into a habit of thinking that mediocrity and dormancy is okay. Becoming a better me, is all about working on myself. I can say I humbly, pursued an intentional journey in October 2018, getting started in The Institute of Marriage and Family Affairs, (TIMFA) Pursuing the Marriage Mentors Certification Course, which I then further advanced to the Marriage Master Mentors Certification Course. Indeed, God had been ordering my steps as I pursued in the area of Marriage getting trained, equipped and to turn my passion into an effective ministry.

God has opened a reservoir for more work to be done when I enrolled in the Mind Renewal Course with the Restoration of the Breach School. Wow! It has been so rewarding. Yes, indeed, here I am in a winning season, writing a chapter about embracing the better me. God is truly Awesome and Amazing.

This Mind Renewal Course is a true expression of perseverance. The course's content is very deep, and I had a lot of work to do each week. I felt like I was a rider on the back of a bike, taking some deep corners. It was a lot of work and certainly deep work in my mind. One thing for sure, I held on, not giving up the ride, ensuring I submitted my assignments on time and put in the work. Some days, I felt so overwhelmed with assignments that I would just cry to God for strength to continue.

Subsequently, I have grown to appreciate the fact that if you want to achieve something, you have to work for it. There is no room for negative thoughts when you are working on yourself.

Remember Proverbs 23:7 *"For as he thinks in his heart, so is he"*. In fact, if you allow negative thoughts to prolong, you will eventually speak negative and of course your life will be negative.

However, because I am intentional about working on myself, I am very mindful of the words I speak. The more I speak God's word, I continually operate with the Mind of Christ. As Philippians 2:5 expresses, *"Let this mind be in you which was also in Christ Jesus"*. I realize that moving to a new mindset is the big key in achieving anything in life. Major construction on the site of my life began when I understood *"Coexisting in the Present and the Future"-Leostone Morrison*...I saw the bright light switch on as I did the introspection and continued taking a look at myself and making the necessary changes.

Working on myself is holistic as it concerns every area of my life. In other words, when I work on myself, I become a better woman, a better wife, and friend, neighbour. Right now, I am embracing the better me. By taking responsibility for who I am becoming I can move out of a mediocre mindset. I have become so tired of the land of mediocrity. The following is also true-working on my life is getting knowledge too. Empowering and equipping myself begins in the mind for sure, developing strong self-confidence, daily remembering what God's Word says about me is my big key. Taking the time out to make declarations of who I am in Christ, in fact it is all about, going forward and taking charge. Yes, I can do all things through Christ who strengthens me. Regardless of the time and season, you can still work on yourself. Since this pandemic, began in 2020 stepping out in bold exploits has become my reality. All my classes I have done online, it started out very challenging but as Joyce Meyer says, "Go after what you want" (excerpt from her book Leader in the Making) I have dismissed procrastination and fear and I have welcomed my new staff, "Faith in God". Hebrews 11:6 expresses this truth; without faith it is impossible to Please God!

Just a few months before I started the Mind Renewal Course, I was busy working on myself by pursuing a Christian Discipleship Programme and the Fundamentals of Biblical Counselling at Whole Life College. Upon completion I was favoured by God to assist with hosting classes online. Glory to God! Because limits have already been demolished, I walked through the open door that God had provided-Victory Breakthrough Carpet rolled out as I continued to seize every opportunity presented so I could work on myself.

In other words, in the land where you renew your mind, there is no place for parking. Have you ever been there? Well today you can get that opportunity to get your mind renewed, oh yes! you can maximize your full potential in God. Take note, that your life is a journey and that means you are always on the move. There is no turning back, now! You have to keep on going. Remember, to get to the Promised Land you will have to navigate your way through the wilderness. Certainly, you will encounter obstacles, problems, challenges across your path but the way you respond to them is one of the most important decisions you will make. Do not give up! Whatever obstacles or dilemmas that you may encounter; have faith in God. Whenever a believer is inactive in their spiritual growth and development, they eventually become immobilized.

Things have really changed a lot in my life when I began the course. Additionally, I must speak about the vision board that we were asked to do. In fact, it was a great challenge to get it done, but it helped me deeply in organising what I want to attain. Seriously, I have never done a vision board before and I embraced it greatly. The truth is, writing a book was also written on my vision board. Now look at what the Lord has done!

Let me encourage you, if you do not have a vision board, get one. Go ahead and write the vision that you have. It is attainable with God's help. The truth is, without a vision, you really do not have a clear path. Working on myself continues with my desire to improve and change my way of thinking. I am pursuing the following: our weekly Prayer Partner Link up, managing my time better, walking in submission to my husband, being that beacon of Christ in my community and workplace, getting physically active as I do my physical work out three evenings per week. No belittling or doubting of self around here. Working on myself is the way to go.

It is a continuous journey, and I am pursuing it with Faith. This is my "Go for it season".

MAKING NEW YEAR'S RESOLUTIONS (my thoughts)

I do believe there is value in making a New Year's Resolution. Many people end up with a long to-do list without thinking deeply. However, if you are purposeful and committed to what you plan to do, it can be achieved. Notwithstanding the obstacles, a better you will mean failing and restarting. I think you should take responsibility for your actions and set a specific goal.

RESOLUTIONS

1. For many years every January my resolution was, 'start exercising more'. However, that never materialized because I kept putting it off making excuses and feeling lazy.

After revisiting the plan, "I committed to working out three times per week so I can be more alert and energized in my body that then, being a specific goal, I began making progress.

2. Another resolution was, "Save money ". That became a reality when I committed to saving five thousand ($5000JMD) per paycheck and that became a WOW when I was able to pay tuition fees for my son. Indeed, you MUST be committed to your commitment.

As you renew your mind you must be honest with yourself about the positives (*Mind Renewal: Biblical Secrets To A Better You* -page 97).

LETTER TO ME

Dear Donna,

Hope you are doing well today! Since you have begun doing this Mind Renewal course, I must say things are really looking good so far. But I want to encourage you to take it a step further. As a child of God, there is always greater in His kingdom. Let me encourage you to always strive to be better, which can only take place in the mind. It is now time to unlock the wealth of your mind and become the better version of yourself.

Yes, Donna, you can be a better mother, wife, Christian, friend, neighbour, and employee. Greatness is in you woman of God. Certainly, now is the time to step into becoming a better version of yourself. Do not procrastinate any longer or allow fear and limitations to hold you back. You are a Victor. Always remember the change begins with your mindset! Look at this. Your feet cannot go anywhere that your mind has not been. Today is the day to MOVE TO A NEW MINDSET. It will not be easy to get there but it is possible. Certainly, there will be challenges with failures and successes, encounters with persons who may propel you or even try to hinder you from becoming a better version of yourself. However, do not be distracted but keep on striving, Ambassador Donna...Let the unique you be expressed by being honest about the positives and the negatives. Know who you are in Christ! Fearfully and wonderfully made, that is who you are. Embracing Mind Renewal and partnering with the Holy Spirit makes pursuing a better Donna possible.

The world is waiting to meet the renewed you. Have a good day.

Yours truly
Donna Morris
The Better Me

MAINTAINING RENEWAL

Foreseen challenges can come against the fulfilment of this new mindset. The fact that God is a God of mega breakthroughs, and victories, I am assured He will take care of me. Sometimes a bit of nervousness tries to creep in, but I lean on God in faith with a renewed mind. With His strength, I can bravely declare the Word of God.! Whenever thoughts of doubt come to my mind, I find myself leaning on God's word about who I am in Him. I am no longer a slave to fear, I am a child of God. No more a servant of sin. Romans 6:6 expresses this powerful truth *"Knowing this, that our old man is crucified with him, that the body of sin might be destroyed, that henceforth we should not serve sin."*

In challenging ourselves to become better, we must maintain this renewal. Stay in the Word of God, and be alert, in the event that the old you come knocking at your door.

143

I really do not have it all together, I am still a work in progress. God is still working on me. Thoughts do sometimes pop up in my mind saying, it is too late to be great, and that I am not needed. In fact, The Word of God has always come to rescue my mind, Glory to God. It is a quick response to those thoughts that seek to exalt themselves against the knowledge of God. Thank you, Lord! With the war between the spirit and the flesh, you can rise to conquer and cast down negative thoughts.

No longer will I allow negative thoughts to be parked in my mind and become a resident. All tenants of doubt, fear and limitations have been put out. According to 2 Corinthians 10: 5, *"it reads," Casting down imaginations, and every high thing that exalteth itself against the knowledge of God, and bringing into captivity every thought to the obedience of Christ"*

As I embrace this new season of my life, being a better me, foreseen challenges could arise to draw me back to consider what people think or say. Well with that thought, it is that moment of worship for me, and meditating on what God's Word says about me. Now is the time for activation of purpose. Notice what is said in Philippians 3:13-14 *"Brethren, I count not myself to have apprehended: but this one thing I do, forgetting those things which are behind, and reaching forth unto those things which are before, I press toward the mark for the prize of the high calling of God in Christ Jesus."*

Look what the Lord has done since I started this course!! AWESOME and AMAZING GOD INDEED!! MIND RENEWAL REALLY LOOKS GOOD ON ME.

THE BETTER ME IS BEING POLISHED BY THE MIGHTY HAND OF GOD... THINGS ARE ALREADY BETTER!! I am walking free from thoughts of REJECTION. IT is a new day over here! I have God's spoken Word in my heart, and it is manifesting.... Thank You JESUS!! I AM

FEELING THE RENEWED ME... I AM WALKING NEW... IT IS ALREADY DONE. Whatever God has started he will complete Philippians 1:6

THE BETTER YOU IS BEAUTIFUL

1. Avoid the temptation to be busily seeing the faults of others so that you begin to see yourselves as angels. No one is perfect, only God. As you become a better you, it is indeed time for introspection, yes look at yourself, not others, and see how you can make that change for the better. However, with this better you coming forth, you can start reflecting on the fact that making the world a better place, really begins with you making a change in your thinking. No finger pointing at others. Personal mind renewal is imperative.

2. A better you will mean failing and restarting. In challenging ourselves to be better, it is a journey that includes failure and successes. Keep on pressing on, do not give up! You may begin a task or a project, do not quit on the journey. Being a finisher is key in becoming a better you.

3. Persevere, learn from your mistakes and move forward in God's grace. Always bear in mind that *you can do all things through Christ who gives you strength (Philippians 4:13).*

4. Walking in forgiveness is a must as you embrace the better you. The only way you can receive forgiveness is by forgiving others. If you do not forgive you will be walking in defeat. The Word of God is clear on this truth about forgiving others, in Mark 11:26, it reads. *"But if ye do not*

forgive, neither will your Father which is in heaven forgive your trespasses" Mark 11:26.

5. It is necessary to take responsibility and accept your errors in life. Do not cast blame on others. The blame game will not help. If your parents could not afford it, now is the time to go back to school; blaming them or others will not make you better.

CHAPTER 8
PURSUING PURPOSE

"For I know the thoughts that I think toward you, saith the Lord, thoughts of peace, and not of evil, to give you an expected end". (Jeremiah 29:11)

In understanding Mind Renewal, it is imperative to note that you must always fulfil purpose. Undoubtedly, God is a God of winning strategies, and He has great and amazing plans for your life. If you remain mindful of the fact that God has created you with the idea that you must maximize your full potential, then you will begin to live your life with great meaning. The question is. "What is a divine purpose"?

A divine purpose is God's calling on someone's life. However, if you do not know God's purpose for your life, you will constantly feel a sense of aimlessness.

149

Today, many individuals are not living their lives on purpose. The truth is that you need to find out what your purpose is and fulfil it. Now is not the time to undermine your potential and doubt what you are capable of achieving. As Mark 10:27 tells us; *"With men it is impossible, but not with God: for with God all things are possible"*. You can fulfil purpose. Are you willing and ready to move from that place of limits, complacency, and fears? Therefore, if you are serious about fulfilling God's purpose in your life, you must begin by exercising your faith by making bold steps to pursue what God has for you.

However, look at what Abraham did in Genesis 12: 1-3. His first move was to step out in faith. Abraham obeyed the Lord as he received the instruction. He was not hesitant to venture into the unknown in pursuit of what God had planned for him.

"Now the Lord had said unto Abram, get thee out of thy country, and from thy kindred, and from thy father's house, unto a land that I will shew thee: And I will make of thee a great nation, and I will bless thee, and make thy name great; and thou shalt be a blessing: And I will bless them that bless thee, and curse him that curseth thee: and in thee shall all families of the earth be blessed. So, Abram departed, as the Lord had spoken unto him; and Lot went with him: and Abram was seventy and five years old when he departed out of Haran".

Pay attention to what I am saying here, let nothing derail you off course, unbelief, fears, and thoughts of limitations can forfeit your destiny. I believe Abraham may have experienced some obstacles in making that step of faith, but the good thing was that he kept his eyes on the call of God.

Yes! You have God's permission to take that step of faith.

As you renew your Mind, **BELIEVE THAT YOUR POTENTIAL IS UNLIMITED.**

As long as you keep your renewed mind fixed on God, you will see Him revealing that a better version of you is waiting to emerge. Let us be honest, your inclination to choose to believe that you are limited does come to your mind. In those moments when I personally choose to think I am limited it was all about relaxing in mind prison. You can also view it as a kind of cave too, that is dark and lonely, but there you need to get out NOW!! No purpose can be fulfilled in that kind of environment. The truth is, there is no one to blame for this, but yourself. Remember there is a reservoir in you. You are filled to the brim with great purposes, wealth of creativity, empowerment, limitless potential. Your Potential is unlimited in God.

However, let me reiterate, do not let your circumstances, where you come from or what people think about you, stop you from fulfilling God's purpose for your life. You, too, can have a story to tell if you believe God's word.

THERE IS ALWAYS PURPOSE IN YOUR PAIN

Purpose does not mean there is no pain. However, despite what you are experiencing, you must always, ask God what He is trying to communicate through the situation. Whatever you may be going through always have a purpose. No one can fulfil that purpose for you. The difficulties in my life's journey have proven to me that as you go through the pain, there is a great purpose at the end, and with all that said, I was fortunate to have a mother who loved me through those times. She offered great encouragement, never to give up.

Even in the most difficult and challenging times of your life you should stop asking God to take away your pain. Despite the aches and pain that you may go through, do not allow the enemy to count you out, there is always a hidden purpose while going through the bruising of life.

Be encouraged, you are not alone in pursuing your purpose. Others have gone through and have come out victorious.

Most importantly, understand that this journey is not for the faint hearted, it requires that you stay in the fight of keeping your faith. The scripture exhorts *"Let us endure hardship as a true soldier of Christ" (2 Timothy 2:3-5).* The enemy knows that you are filled with great wealth of potential and he wants to disinherit you, hence he seeks to undermine you.

As believers your attitude in pain, must certainly announce purpose!!! There is the pain of disobedience and the pain of obedience! Always bear in mind that even though it may be painful to obey God. The greater pain stems from being disobedient. Consequently, Jonah as recorded in the scripture paid greatly for not walking in the instruction he was given by the Lord, and he faced the consequences of disobedience. It is important to stay in the will of God for your life, so that purpose can be fulfilled.

Now is the time to embrace moving to a new mindset and walk into divine purpose.

When I reflect on the journey of renewing the mind, I have always encountered the key to forgiveness. It is importantly shared throughout this book. There is no way you can fulfil divine purpose and walk in unforgiveness. It is a big hindrance in getting where God wants you. Forgiveness of oneself and others is very crucial in discovering that divine purpose which the Lord has for you. Do you want to open the gates of your own mind? Then Forgive.

We should not stop being kind and considerate toward others. That is the renewed you and because of what the Lord has done in your life. Please do not allow people to drag you down to the level where you become unforgiving.

No matter how they make you feel, do not render evil for evil and harbour bitterness in your heart. However, do not be afraid to allow the Holy Spirt to reveal any unforgiveness in your heart towards others. Remember you are on the path to pursue purpose. Wow! That is a totally different road right there. As God's Image bearer you must guard your focus, as you are on the path of freedom. Some people will never like you just because you are pursuing a life of purpose. No matter how you are even serving them. With that said, do not let that deter you, Carry on anyway. Remember you are purpose driven by God and he expects you to act like it.

Forgiveness and pursuing purpose is a big choice. However, you are not forced to practice it. You are simply called to exhibit it that it brings glory and honour to God. Whatever choices you make you will be rewarded for the same. Your Heavenly Father will forgive you when you forgive others. The gospel of Mark puts it well:

"But if ye do not forgive, neither will your Father which is in heaven forgive your trespasses." *(Mark 11:26)*

You are making that choice to fulfil purpose!!

PRAY MORE

The most important thing you can do in life as you pursue your purpose is to keep praying. The more you engage in prayer, it is guaranteed that you will become intimate with God. Praying more will reveal   to you that you are building a strong relationship with the Lord. Being a praying Christian is to be a powerful Christian.

157

Prayerlessness is a big problem among many believers. In fact, it is often discovered that persons who do not pray consistently are often in a much-weakened spiritual state. On the other hand, no one needs to tell you that you are God's creation, and he has a purpose for you being here. So, whatever you do in life, you must always communicate with him. The Bible clearly states that it is very important to commune with God in prayer. It teaches in 2 Chronicles 7:14, how His people are to approach Him. *"If my people, which are called by my name, shall humble themselves, and pray and seek my face, and turn from their wicked ways, then will I hear from heaven, and will forgive their sin, and will heal their land"*. Obviously, if you want God to move on your behalf, your answer is to pray more. The scripture in 2 Chronicles 7 outlines that once there is a lack of prayer, things will always deteriorate. The more time you spend in prayer; the more you must be on guard to be humble. As you pursue purpose, you must constantly seek God's face, and be ready and open to hear what He has to say and commune with him regularly. Undoubtedly, God is big on fellowship, and so man is made for fellowship with God.

"And they heard the voice of the LORD God walking in the garden in the cool of the day: and Adam and his wife hid themselves from the presence of the LORD God amongst the trees of the garden. And the LORD God called unto Adam, and said unto him, where art thou?" (Genesis 3:8-9)

If you want to maintain fellowship in prayer, you must repent from sin and pursue the ways of God. Most importantly, spending more time with God will allow you to be more sensitive to the leadings of The Spirit of God. Let me urge you to keep yourself covered with prayer, as you move forward in moving to a new mindset. You ought to spend time in prayer so the Lord can speak to

159

you. Remember praying is a two-way street, and so praying without ceasing should be the position of your heart.

THE GOD OF A SECOND CHANCE

God is truly awesome, and He has great plans and purposes for us. He had such a great purpose for Minister Stacey Ann Garvey, and she was not afraid to expose the scars in her life. She shared her story of God's overwhelming love holding on to her tightly and never letting her go. I am impressed by the power of God in her life and to see God's deliverance from a physical prison and a prison of the mind. This purposeful vessel of God could not die. Regardless of her mess, God has a great message to broadcast to the world at large. God found her behind the prison bars; she experienced loads of depression, rejection, abortions, suicidal thoughts, revelling tattooing, so many painful experiences but God showed up miraculously on her behalf. Min. Garvey expressed that she felt like a dry bone that was thrown in a valley, and that her pain is her wealth. Wow! This is so powerful; certainly, this is evidence of a mind that has been moved to a new mindset. When you see the great transformation work of deliverance that took place, in her life you can join with the Psalmist in Psalms 126:3 that says: *"The LORD hath done great things for us; whereof we are glad."*

Looking at this Mighty Woman of God; she is indeed a Purpose Carrier.

Even with that prison experience, Min. Stacy Garvey received a prison break from a mediocre mind! Her testimony exposes the lies of the enemy and reveals the work of the Holy Spirit in her heart.

God has given her a second chance to live, and today she is definitely living her life on purpose.

Glory to God! While she was incarcerated, she listened to the Word of God preached by a visiting pastor. He preached on the sermon topic, "Do not let the devil end your story." Min. Garvey's story could not be terminated by the enemy! The truth is, everything she had gone through had a ministry attached; there is so much beauty in her scars. The Word of God is life transforming and it always echoes PURPOSE.

VICTORY is on display here. Glory to God!

The devil had to SHUT UP because he cannot kill what God has anointed to live.

PURPOSE IN SAUL'S LIFE (Acts 9)

As we examine the life of the Apostle Paul, we will begin to see that he had to go through the process of becoming a chosen vessel. Even though Saul was uttering threats with every breath and he was eager to kill God's people, he was still chosen by God.

162

The enemy may have tried to abort it, but it just could not work. In spite of the attacks on your life, bear in mind that chosen vessels endure great attacks. God had a big plan and purpose for Saul's life to glorify Him and spread the gospel of Jesus Christ, and it had to manifest. While on his own mission, on the road to Damascus, God had to give him an encounter in the form of a light from heaven. There he fell on his face, and his name was called out' *"Saul, Saul why persecutest thou me"?*

Saul was blinded in this instance but thank God for his destiny helpers who led him by the hand into Damascus. Paul endured a lot of struggles throughout his life, it began when he was converted. Regardless of the circumstances, it is very clear to me that when you meet Jesus, you will find the purpose for your life. Saul got the revelation of his purpose, soon after that moment on Damascus Road and he never turned back. No matter how terrible and murderous a person maybe, God can still use them-purpose MUST be fulfilled.

Let us look at a few of the struggles Paul had to face in his life, even as he was pursuing purpose. Like Paul, you should be determined to finish your course.

In Damascus they laid wait to slay him *(Acts 9:29)*.

In Iconium they attempted to stone him *(Acts 14:5)*.

In Lystra they stoned him and left him to die *(Acts 14:19)*.

And in Philippi they beat him and put him in stocks *(Acts 16:23-24)*.

The scripture went on to state that while he was in prison, he prayed and sang praises unto God *(Acts 16:25)*.

God takes purpose very seriously, and he wants us to take it seriously too. Saul had to submit to the hand of God in his life, even as he went through his fiery circumstances. As you renew your mind, take into consideration that submission is key in fulfilling purpose. Be open to this truth that we cannot negotiate with God about our mission.

AM I PURSUING MY CALLING?

1 Peter 4:10: "As every man hath received the gift, even so minister the same one to another, as good stewards of the manifold grace of God."

Glory to God, what a blessing it is to know that Christ, the Redeemer, the Holy One of Israel is living in me. I am valuable, loved and extremely special to God, He calls me His peculiar treasure, so here I am embracing God's call on my life, by making that choice to pursue purpose!!

The question was asked, "Am I pursuing my calling?" I responded in the affirmative from my humbly perspective, knowing that God is calling me to operate in faith.

For sure God has orchestrated everything in the MIND RENEWAL COURSE to keep me going.

It does not matter the challenges, but with God's grace assisting me. I will remain faithful and obedient to Him. The Lord has brought me through many things so that I can receive the blessings that He has in store for me. Consequently, as I unlock the wealth of my mind and begin to live intentionally, I can truly embrace what is stated in *Colossians 3:23: "Whatever I have been called to do, I will do it heartily unto the Lord and not unto men".*

I have been called to mentor others, encourage, study the Word of God, serve, and help others in hospitality and leadership. Such a wonderful

166

feeling to know that God's Word can be on display in my life.

With God's grace I will continue to submit to his leadership to serve in my callings, making impact as I reflect Christ likeness and bear the fruit of the Spirit. So, whatever I am called to do, I let God do what needs to be done from my inside out. With the various callings in my life, I commit to read, study the Word of God, pray, fast, and research. Allocate time in my day to connect with others locally or internationally, whether with a text message, an email, a phone call or just a pleasant smile or hello. Giving up is never an option, as I know that God has orchestrated my life so I can impact those that come across my path. Whatever I have been called to do, by the Grace of God I will press on in confidence. My life is being lived on purpose; I am here to make a difference for the Lord. *"If I Can Help Somebody" -Mahalia Jackson* has brought forth a great message through this song. It was one of my mother's favourites.

"If I can help somebody, as I travel along
If I can help somebody, with a word or song.
If I can help somebody, from doing wrong,
No, my living shall not be in vain"

To someone who is reading this, I encourage you to use your gifting and talents and ask God for directions. Ask Him to identify His purpose or calling for your life and He will provide the answers and lead you to it.

KEY POINTS IN PURSUING PURPOSE

1. COMPLACENCY IS AN ENEMY TO DIVINE PURPOSE.

It is very important that you know what your assignments are and do not become complacent. You must serve God wholeheartedly and experience wow seasons.

168

2. GOD STRATEGICALLY PUTS US IN POSITION, WE ARE NOT HERE BY ACCIDENT.

You are certainly here on purpose to make an impact in your family, in your church, and workplace. God's purpose in your life must be fulfilled everywhere you go.

3. GOD INTENTS FOR YOU TO IMPACT INFLUENCE AND COLONIZE.

Certainly, God's plan for you, as you occupy the earth, is that you become impactful in how you serve others and serve Him.

4. RUN YOUR LEG OF THE JOURNEY, BE UNIQUE IN RUNNING.

Be yourself. Do not try to be like anyone. You are handpicked to do what you do. When God has selected you, it does not matter who else has rejected or neglected you. God's favour outweighs all opposition.

169

5. WHEN YOU LIVE ON PURPOSE MORE PEOPLE WILL BE IMPACTED.

Others are always blessed when you are fulfilling your purpose. As long as you know your purpose, then you should go forth and fulfil it. Once you get up and go, your purpose will be fulfilled.

6. STOP ASKING GOD TO TAKE AWAY THE PAIN.

Embrace the journey as you go towards fulfilling your purpose. Always remember you must be willing to go through pain. Do not pray it away.

7. PURPOSE DOES NOT MEAN THERE IS NO PAIN.

Ask God what is the purpose in your pain. Pay attention to your attitude in the pain, because out of pain comes purpose.

8. EXCELLENCE IS NOT ON BREAK.

Whatever you do for God must always be done in excellence. It does not matter the circumstances that you may be facing, you should always honor God.

The Lord must get the best worship, even when you are financially challenged.

9. YOUR ATTITUDE SHOULD NOT ALTER BECAUSE OF THE SEASON YOU ARE IN.

Always pay attention to your attitude when you have difficult seasons. Your lives are impacting others, just by the way you react when you are in unpleasant moments. You should serve with such great excellence; because you do not know who you are impacting.

10. PRACTICE STRATEGIC EVANGELISM, IMPACT PERSONS BY THE WAY WE LIVE.

People are taking note of the way you serve. Murmuring and complaining about everything not going your way is often observed by people around us.

Moving to a new mindset is all about unlocking the wealth of your mind. Pursue whatever career path you have always wanted; blaming others will not make things better. The world is definitely awaiting the better you.

CHAPTER 9
SLAY THE GOLIATH

Let us face it. We all have goliaths. Some are real and some are in our imagination. It is imperative to note that even as you pursue a life of great purpose, God will always empower you to slay the giants that seek to intimidate you. However, as you journey through life, you will realize that God has also destined you to live a life of great faith, and not to be crippled by fear. My journey in Mind Renewal continues to expose the many goliaths that I have faced and today, I can report great victory in Jesus' name! I could never have faced them all by myself. My true reality is that I have confronted many goliaths and conquered them through the power of the Lord.

What type of goliath are you facing in this season of your life? Think about it. You may have faced different goliaths in your life. Some of those challenges can be a medical diagnosis, unemployment, financial struggles, divorce, dealing with an unresolved issue with someone, struggling with a job situation. However, faith and trust in God will see you through. Sometimes the goliath that you face has been initiated by God, as a part of your faith-building and character-building plan. However, God knows that the goliath you are facing is able to bring Him glory. In contrast, some of the adversities you face because of a goliath type situation can also be initiated by the enemy because he wants to frustrate, intimidate, hinder, and get you to become fearful and unbelieving. Remember without faith it is impossible to please God. Therefore, you must always activate faith when you face goliaths.

Jesus Himself said that nothing would be impossible if you believe. Therefore, do you believe that you can slay every goliath that comes your way? It is indeed possible as long as you are connected to a God who is Omnipotent.

There are many goliaths that exist, but thankfully you can have access to prayer and God's Word to slay them in Jesus' Mighty name. Few Christians realize that the presence of God in their lives and the infallible word of God is a reservoir of wealth, encouragement, and power. I am writing this chapter out of a deep desire to help those who believe that they must suffer defeat from goliaths, and do not know how to slay them. As you move to a new mindset hold to this truth: We are in a spiritual warfare and therefore you can only use spiritual weapons to defeat the enemy or the goliath that faces you.

THE ATTACK BEGINS IN THE MIND

The enemy's number one place to attack you is in your mind. He begins the war in our thoughts, and so we will begin to think that the challenge we are facing is some enormous giant that cannot be defeated. Thoughts always invade your mind concerning any situation to bring on doubt and unbelief, however scripture expresses that you should be renewed in the spirit of your mind (Ephesians 4:23).

In 2019, I got a letter from a utility company concerning some outstanding payments. The moment I opened the letter I was gripped with fear because I had no money to clear it. Additionally, I was given a few days to settle the arrears. Can I tell you, the first feeling that came was worry? That was so paralyzing because different thoughts began to flood my mind. All of this happened so fast, I could literally feel a spirit of depression coming over me. Let me tell you this, the attack on the mind is a real thing!

I recall one of my church sisters called me on the phone, just about the same moment. That is how on time God works! Glory to God! Yes! The Holy

176

Spirit stepped in to intercede on my behalf. Literally, I felt like the biggest goliath was standing in front of me at that time, and I had no idea what to do. It is very crippling when fearful thoughts arrest the mind. It literally immobilizes you and causes you to feel stuck.

Look how God showed up for me. That was definitely a destiny helper moment. Immediately as my church sister began to pray and declare the word of God over me, I felt courage swept into my heart, I declared boldly *"God is my refuge and strength a very present help in the time of trouble"*. Upon declaring the Word of truth and praying, that was the moment I slayed that goliath.

The Apostle Paul states in 2 Corinthians 10:4 that; *"the weapons of our warfare are not carnal, but mighty through God to the pulling down of strong holds"*. See what I am saying here? The area of our thoughts is a battlefield" You ought to watch out! Let me reiterate that the war begins in the mind. In the next verse, 2 Corinthians 10: 5, it speaks of *"casting down imaginations, and every high thing that exalts itself against the knowledge of God, bringing every thought into captivity to the obedience of Christ"*.

YOU MUST HAVE THE MIND OF CHRIST

It is very important that Christians have the mind of Christ. As the Bible says in Philippians 2:5; *"Let this mind be in you which was also in Christ Jesus"*. With that being said, I have seen fewer Christians pay attention in guarding the mind. They fill their minds with television, social media, secular music, internet websites, newspaper articles, video games and conversations of the world. If you do not invest in the renewing of the mind, then thousands of thoughts will invade the mind that concerns the things of the world. The Bible cautions us that the carnal mind in itself is enmity against God, so when we read the Word of God and meditate on it, it gets into our minds and goes down into our spirits (Romans 8:7). The more time you invest in doing this, you will see transformation taking place in your life. God wants you to be active about transformation. Therefore, it is imperative that you invest in getting Bibles, books and relevant material to build up your faith. As vividly as I remember, my friend Donna Rhoden and I would be intentional about going to the bookstore. It has been a journey over the years as we pursued mind renewal. Of course, it cost us money. In fact, every investment has to do with money. However, we invested in our renewing of the mind project by buying Bibles, ordering books online and getting material concerning the Word of God to build our faith. Bear in mind that once you engage your mind with God's truth, you will receive the power to choose which thoughts you entertain in your mind and which ones you cast down. In other words, you will begin to see things from

God's perspective. You must have the mind of Christ to face every goliath.

No matter how big your goliath is, you can face it with God. As you experience the renewing of the mind, do not panic when you encounter various types of goliaths. However, all you need to do is to confront them and slay them. That may sound easy, but it certainly requires a commitment to walk with God, and by all means you will be slaying goliaths. So, prepare yourself to get into prayer and allow the Word of God to dwell in you richly. The Bible tells us that the weapons with which you do spiritual warfare are not weapons of this world... instead they are spiritual weapons that God has given us, they have divine power to demolish satanic strongholds (2 Corinthians 10:4-5).

A life of faith in Christ is a life that will have conflict. Therefore, you will always have opposition from the enemy. As you move to a new mindset, I encourage you not to be afraid.

David was certainly not afraid to address the goliath that was standing in front of him, consequently he was not intimidated, *"And David spake to the men that stood by him, saying, what shall be done to the man that killeth this Philistine, and taketh away the reproach from Israel? For who is this uncircumcised Philistine, that he should defy the armies of the living God?"* (1 Samuel 17:26)

Like David, most of us have faced a goliath at some time or the other, that big uncircumcised philistine with a spear and shield that seems so threatening to our lives.

Look how equipped David was. He was standing in the name of the Lord of Hosts!! *"Then said David to the Philistine, thou comest to me with a sword, and with a spear, and with a shield: but I come to thee in the name of the LORD of hosts, the God of*

181

the armies of Israel, whom thou hast defied. (1 Samuel 17:45)

"This day will the LORD deliver thee into mine hand; and I will smite thee, and take thine head from thee; and I will give the carcases of the host of the Philistines this day unto the fowls of the air, and to the wild beasts of the earth; that all the earth may know that there is a God in Israel. And all this assembly shall know that the LORD saveth not with sword and spear: for the battle is the LORD's, and he will give you into our hands". (1 Samuel 17: 46-47)

David's mind was definitely focused on his God, knowing that He is able. In fact, when David spots the target moving towards him, he seizes the moment to take him down. Right now, you may be experiencing thoughts of fear, doubt and worry, but I encourage you to hold on to your faith. Do not retreat or hide from your goliath. In other words, start thinking about slaying him. As you renew your mind, be conscious that even though a six-cubit giant stands in front of you, begin to celebrate this victory in Jesus' name. This was a very important God moment for David, so he made use of the opportunity to take a victory stone from his bag, slung it and struck Goliath in the forehead. *"Immediately he fell face down on the ground" (1 Samuel 17:49).*

Giants are everywhere and with the mind of Christ, you can load your sling and slay that goliath in your life. Giants such as rejection, fear, depression, stress, mediocrity. You can boldly declare the Word of the Lord and say, "you will not conquer me, I am not afraid, but I will slay you and cut off your head". Remember, God is your defense and you do not have to fear. It is time to win the battle in your mind and you will be able to run boldly toward freedom. Obviously, what God gave David, he gave you too.

There is no doubt that God has equipped you and He will fight for you. Instead of running away or having a pity party about how big your giant is, it is time to stand and face that goliath. It is time to be empowered by the authority you have been given through Jesus. There is no room for fear when you are dealing with goliaths. Regardless of how big they look; remember you are trained for this battle. You are courageous, full of faith and have the mind of Christ. According to 2 Tim 1:7; *"For God hath not given us the spirit of fear, but of power and of love and of a sound mind".*

Looking through the lens of a renewed mind, I can see all giants in my life as defeated foes. The truth is you can slay them and walk in victory in the name of the Lord. The more time you spend with God and get into His Word, you will be better able to identify thoughts of fear when you see them approaching your mind.

Today you have power to demolish thoughts that want you to retreat from your goliath challenges.

Take authority over them and cut off the head in Jesus' name.

CONFESS THE WORD IN PRAYER AND SLAY GOLIATHS

Confessing the Word of God in prayer should be an important part of every believer's life when facing spiritual warfare.

In Ephesians 6:17-18, it states, *"And take the helmet of salvation, and the sword of the Spirit, which is the word of God, praying always with all prayer and supplication in the Spirit, and watching thereunto with all perseverance and supplication for all saints"*. In the scripture passage shared from Ephesians 6, it is clearly identified that the Sword of the Spirit and prayer are vital ammunitions to be used in spiritual battles. I have never discovered a more powerful way of demolishing strongholds and goliaths than praying scripture. Indeed, the scriptures have brought so much wealth to the mind, I can say without a doubt that it is

185

transformational. Remember, the renewing of your mind is an intentional journey, and it must be pursued with diligence. I am a living proof that God can use an imperfect clay pot and make it valuable. As I conclude this chapter of the book: I have included some scripture-prayers below. You will be immensely blessed as you search for the scripture reference in your Bible.

Father in the name of Jesus, thank you for renewing my mind.

Sovereign Lord, you are able to do great and mighty things.

Lord, I know you have great power and nothing is impossible with you. (Jeremiah 32:17)

Spirit of the Living God, guard our minds from all arrows of past hurts in Jesus' name! *"Your right hand is glorious in power; your right-hand o Lord shatters the enemy" (Exodus 15:6)*

Father in the name of Jesus, thank you Lord for the shield of victory, to slay all goliaths, arm us with strength and make our adversary bow at our feet in Jesus mighty name. (Psalms 18:35-36 39, 40)

Thank you, Lord, for helping us to maximize our fullest potential as we fulfil our purpose, bless us and surround us with favour like a shield. (Psalms 5:12)

In the name of Jesus, we receive divine thoughts, revelations, wisdom and understanding, as we stand on the Word of God. (Psalms 119:89)

Help us Lord to let go of past hurts, and to receive your peace as we walk in freedom in our minds. (Isaiah 26:3)

Mighty God empower us to bear with others and practice walking in forgiveness in Jesus' name. (Colossians 3:13)

In Jesus name when you let go of the past, all fear will go and you will walk in faith, because you are an *Ambassador of the Lord Jesus Christ. (2 Corinthians 5:20)*

Mighty God, you are our light and salvation. You are the strength of our life, and there is no need to fear anything or anyone in Jesus' mighty name. (Psalms 27:1)

Heavenly Father, thank you for the deliverance from an impoverished mind, because of Your favour the enemy will not triumph over us (Psalms 41:11)

Omnipotent God, we cancel every weapon of the enemy that has been formed to affect the mind (Isaiah 54:17)

On the authority of your Word, we declare that through God we shall do valiantly, and tread down our enemies. (Psalms 108:13)

Thank you, Lord, for redeeming us from the curse of limitations, rejections, fears, and making us more than a conqueror. (Galatians 3:13, Romans 8:37)

Gracious Father, we will not call to our mind the former things of the past. In Jesus' name, we look for the newness, it shall spring forth! Hallelujah Lord, we embrace this new mindset and what the Lord will do. (Isaiah 43:18-19)

CHAPTER 10
NEW MINDSET

It is said a journey of a thousand miles starts with one step. I believe this was a step of faith, on December 31, 2020, when I was introduced to the nine weeks Mind Renewal Course offered by the Restoration of the Breach school. It was announced at my church watch night Thanksgiving Service that was held on a zoom platform. I am so grateful to the Holy Spirit for that nudge to get registered in the course even though the thoughts lingered whether I should enrol in the program. I took the courage to make the move of faith. The truth is, God made the provision by sending the funds to pay for the course, way ahead of time. It was a special birthday gift sent by a special friend. Can I tell you? My journey to moving to a new mindset started off with an uncommon financial favour.

Registering to do The Mind Renewal Course was a right on time blessing that has empowered me for exploits. Regardless of what is happening in our nation and our world, every step you take towards fulfilling your purpose to becoming a better person makes you feel happier, more confident and fulfilled.

A NEW MINDSET ALWAYS TAKES YOU FORWARD!!!

Yes, indeed a forward move is exactly what I have experienced through my journey of moving to a new mindset. It is with great thrill that I can share with you about this new mindset. It impacts your thoughts; it is your compass through which you do life. The Bible clearly states that for a life to be transformed, a mind must be renewed. It is beautifully expressed in Romans 12:2; *"And be not conformed to this world but be ye transformed by the renewing of your mind, that ye may prove what is that good, and acceptable, perfect, will of God"*. There is no other way a new mindset can take place, if you are intentional about changing your mind. With a new mind set you will certainly be a better person too and your life will be much better. However, whenever your actions are changing, it is always a result of your thinking. A new way of thinking can only be acquired through the Word of God. The truth is that every other way of thinking is not as effective as God's promises. To adequately renew your mind, you must be willing to receive the Word of God and let it become a lifestyle. The Word of truth that is so powerful as stated in Hebrews 4 :12; *"For the Word of God is quick and powerful and sharper than any two-edged sword, piercing even to the dividing asunder of soul and spirit, and of the joints and marrow, and is a discerner of the thoughts and intents of the heart"*.

Many people are not aware of the effectiveness of the Sword of the Spirit which is the Word of God and what it can do. In fact, it is guaranteed

192

to give you good success, good health, and everything that you need to move forward in your life. Here is what Joshua says, *"This book of the law shall not depart out of thy mouth, but thou shalt mediate therein day and night, that thou mayest observe to do according to all that is written therein; for then thou shalt have good success"*. So as long as you stay in the Word of God day and night your transformed mind will become a reality.

If you reflect on the old way of thinking you will see that it is loaded with doubts, limitations, and fears. Bear in mind that your old way of thinking can only take you to a certain level in life. It is called the road of limitations. Let me tell you about the road of limitations. There are a lot of persons on that road and so I felt like I was in a good place while I was there. It is mainly all about being in my comfort zone, enjoying the scenery of life and not wanting to go higher. On the road of limitations, you do not have a vision board, you are just aimlessly doing life. I know what it is like to hold back when I reach certain crossroads, it is like saying "O no Lord, I cannot cross that busy street", when in fact God is saying "it is time to go over on the highway of your faith, because, I have a lot more in store for you". The moment I took my eyes off the environs and begun to focus on what God's Word said about me, as stated in Philippians 4:13; *"I can do all things through Christ who strengthens me", I* began to move in faith from the roads of limitations, I began to make good progress in experiencing moving to a new mindset. Yes! It is a real experience to think of the Word of God! It sure gives Impact. Do you really want to get off the road of limitations? You can start right now by beginning to think about the Word of God and what it says about you. It is just that simple! Remember that Word is able to *pierce soul and spirit. (Hebrews 4:12)* That is exactly what happened to me. What a power in the Word of

God! Right away, something will begin to take place in your life.

Now more than ever, you will see the need for the life transforming word to be embedded in you. God's Word always propels you into a high level of thinking. However, the moment you let go of the old way of thinking and begin to embrace the renewal of the mind, a new mindset will evolve; and your life will begin to take a forward move in contrast to the old mindset that is filled with doubts.

BENEFITS OF A NEW MINDSET

For many decades, the old way of thinking has been dominant as it attaches itself to the minds of persons that they have not been able to fulfil divine purpose. With this positive and renewed mind, you are now able to take charge of your destiny.

As a matter of fact, a new mindset is available for everyone who is willing to let go of the past, expose their scars and stand on the Word of God. It is a wealthy way to live when you choose to live a transformed life and it can begin right now, by changing the way you think. Embark on the path to moving to a new mindset.

No need to procrastinate any longer about moving to a new mindset. Now is the time to move forward and experience the wonderful benefits of a new mindset. Your life will be transformed and certainly move in a new direction.

With you mind being renewed and the transformed you coming forth, you will be thrilled about this new path that the Lord has carved out for you. However, it is a winning season for you, and you made the choice to submit to the Lord and embrace your God designed next move.

To adequately renew your mind, you must be willing to deal with rejection from others, who have refrained from speaking to you as they usually do. Remain calm, stay focused and trust God for what He has in store for you. However, the scaling down has already begun for me. Thank you, Lord, for revealing those who are a part of my new season. Right now, God has already given me the relevant tools to secure my victorious new direction.

With that said, look at your own circumstances. Are you guilty of missing out on the benefits of a new mindset? It is all about a new perspective on your life, God's divine perspective. As you move to a new mindset you will begin to have thoughts that reflect a transformed mind. The way God thinks is much higher than yours. Isaiah 55:8-9 reads; *"For my thoughts are not your thoughts, neither are your ways my ways" saith the Lord, "for as the heavens are higher than the e earth, so are my ways*

197

higher than your ways, and my thoughts your thoughts".

YOU WILL PROSPER

When you move to a new mindset; it will cause you to be fruitful. In fact, you will be like a tree planted in the Word, your leaves will stay fresh and green, and you will prosper.

There is no doubt that you will bring forth fruit in your season and you will always bloom. However, if you renew your mind according to the Word of God, it is guaranteed that you will prosper in all areas of your life. Psalms 1:2-3 gives you great wealth in the scripture concerning what is available. *"But his delight is in the law of the LORD; and in his law doth he meditate day and night". And he shall be like a tree planted by the rivers of water, that bringeth forth his fruit in his season; his leaf also shall not wither; and whatsoever he doeth shall prosper".*

In your Spiritual life, you will prosper.

In your Marriage, you will prosper.

In your health, you will prosper.

In your finances, you will prosper.

Whatever you do, it is guaranteed that you will prosper, and good success will be available to you.

WALK IN FAITH

Another benefit of a new mindset is that you will walk in faith.

A renewed mind always causes you to receive the Word, believe it and walk in it. Suddenly the reality of what the Word of God says has now become a reality as a result of your new mindset. Stepping out of your boat by faith, just like Peter did is exactly what you will do. Stepping out by faith, not knowing where the Lord is taking you like Abraham in Genesis 12 is now your new reality.

When doubters come around you, it will be difficult to speak their language because you have let go of the old mindset. God's grace has brought you thus far and He will help you to keep walking in faith. Now is the time for God's people to get a new pair of faith shoes. The same old way of thinking will not take you very far. Moved to a New Mindset will cause you to experience a new dimension in your life. Great possibilities instead of doubts will be your extraordinary results.

I am thankful to God that the weapons of my warfare are not carnal. Thank you, Lord, for equipping us to deal with any old ugly thought that may come to our mind, seeking to distract us from embracing this new path in renewing our minds. 2 Corinthians 10 reads: *"For the weapons of our warfare are not carnal, but mighty through God to the pulling down of strongholds"*. I am persuaded to pursue my new mindset. Since my mind is being renewed, I am now viewing this new direction in a special way. Philippians 1:6 reminds us that God has begun a good work in us and He will complete it. You can choose to attain it or waste it. You must choose to intentionally push through the limitations of your present circumstances and attain the wealth of your next move. You are preparing to be the best in your new season. Thank you, JESUS, for taking us on the journey to the cross so that we can experience a glorious next. A NEW MINDSET ALWAYS TAKES YOU FORWARD!!!

Praise God, I am confident of my position in Christ, victory is always guaranteed. Hold on to this truth: You have to win in your mind before your new mindset becomes a reality. Now that is an awesome statement. Do not lose the battle in your mind. However, understand from today, that you are an overcomer, and you have the victory over limitations and fears. With your faith shoes buckled on, you can walk in a new dimension of who you are. Pursuing purpose should be your only option right now. You have that option as you stand on the Word of God. Obviously, with a renewed mind, you will triumph over every goliath. 2 Corinthians 2:14 states, *"Now thanks be unto God, which always causeth us to triumph in Christ. And maketh manifest the savour of his knowledge by us in every place"*. Regardless of the size of the giant, with your new mindset, you can slay them. Keep moving in the right direction, start expecting things to change in your favour. The Holy Spirit is always with you on your mind renewal journey. Be bold in standing against all impoverished thoughts, and do not ever settle for a life of mediocrity. The great news is that you can embrace the new mindset that awaits you.

REMEDY FOR MOVING FORWARD

1. LET GO OF THE PAST.

Releasing the past is the remedy for moving forward.

All baggage must be left behind. Forsaking the past could be a broken relationship, failed business, hurts from friends and family; it is now time for you to move forward.

2. YOUR MINDSET WILL BEGIN TO CHANGE AS YOU GO THROUGH THINGS.

 As you go through the different situations in your life, it is possible to experience a new mindset. Take time out to renew your mind, hide God's Word in your heart. Take your thoughts captive to the truth and abide in the Word of God.

3. BE CONTINUOUS IN WORSHIPPING AND PRAYING TO GOD.

You should be faithful in your relationship with the Lord.

This relationship should not be on and off. Let us not be slothful in business, but fervent in spirit in serving the Lord.

4. THERE IS PAIN IN THE WILL OF GOD.

God will come with some deep sacrifice, and you must be willing to go through the pain. Remember as long as you obey God and are willing to trust Him, He will carry you through every painful experience.

5. GOING THROUGH A SEASON OF FAMINE WILL TEACH YOU HOW TO FEED OTHERS.

Having an experience without many resources will certainly give you lessons on how to know exactly what others go through when they are in need or are faced with severe lack.

6. GOD DOES NOT ANSWER PRAYER HOW YOU WANT IT.

God is Sovereign, He is your heavenly Father, and He knows what is best for His children. The Lord's ways are not like yours, but you can trust Him to take care of you.

7. GOD CAN GIVE YOU SOMETHING SOLID IN THE MIDST OF BEING BROKE.

Great Provider, that is who God is; He is more than able to do all things. He can supply every need in the midst of a big financial lack.

8. WE CAN LIVE OUT THE PROMISED WORD THAT GOD HAS GIVEN.

The Promises of God are yours to live by, regardless of the unfavourable conditions, you can still worship God in any situation

205

9. DON'T WORRY ABOUT THE HOW, PURSUE THE NEXT.

God is the source of all resources; trust Him with all your heart as you pursue the next move. Just go for it. The time is now. As you pray and seek God for direction, He will connect you with your destiny helpers.

10. IN THE STATE OF NOTHINGNESS TRUST GOD.

God can make something great out of nothing.

He wants to give you uncommon favours and resources.

Let us keep trusting Him and pursue our next. Trust only Him.

PERSEVERE TO GET THERE

No matter how often you have failed in the past, you can still make that change and improve your life. Growing and developing into the best version of yourself is still possible. As your mind is being moved to a new mindset, hold on to this truth: You are here on purpose and you must persevere in life, never giving up on your dreams and aspirations.

If you give up and accept the defeat of your dreams, you will not fulfil your purpose. No matter what happens in the journey of your life, never give in to despair. Take heart and empower yourself with knowledge. Rise above and beyond the limitations of your mind and PERSEVERE.

You must move forward. You must be like Paul and say, *"I have fought the good fight, I have finished the race, I have kept the faith."*

A few years ago, I did an insurance examination. It was one of those papers that you have to work with a lot of formula to study long and hard to pass. Every time I submitted the answers, I was below the pass mark by just a few points. It was frustrating at the time but one thing I did was to keep my mind on the goal and persevered to get there.   Notwithstanding, I faced doubts and worry along the way, but I was going in a direction that my mind had already gone. Success was awaiting me after doing a resit of the examination. Bearing in mind that failures are temporary realities and should not be overshadowed by excellent exam grades, I forged ahead and was successful in moving to a new mindset victory and good success is guaranteed.

Knowing who you are in Christ is very important in preserving in life... As a child of God, you must know that God has a great plan for your life and when you know who you are in Christ, you will be better able to live your life on purpose as God intended.

God sees your life in its entirety and knows all that it will take to get you to fulfil His will. He knows how He wants the events of our lives to end. He also knows how to position you so that you fulfil His plan and glorify Him. You have been positioned by God. I believe God was setting the stage for me to write this book when I enrolled in the Mind Renewal Course. What a surprise roll out! I am still in awe of how God has organized this victory.

Though the challenges existed I am still persevering to the end. Listen to this, you should never allow the enemy to block your doorway of opportunities with doubt, fears, and low self-esteem. Instead, you must act wisely and obey the Lord's commands. A better version of yourself is on the horizon.

In the account shared in Matthew 14:30, Peter obeyed Christ's instruction to step out and walk by faith.

It is interesting to note that before he stepped out of the boat, he said, *"Lord if it be thou, bid me come unto thee on the water"* And Jesus responded to Peter and said *"Come"*. However, the fact that Peter obeyed, it was the best decision he ever

209

made. The first lesson revealed here in this story is to trust God when He gives you a command. In fact, even if it seems frightening as walking on turbulent water. Just as Peter trusted Jesus to do the impossible, we can trust Jesus to do the impossible in our lives. Walking in obedience to God's Word is always the right thing to do. As you renew your mind, you will discover that God's plan for your life begins with the key to obedience. You will never go wrong obeying God. You may not know where the Lord is taking you but one thing for sure, when you get to the place He has called you to go, you will experience an overflow of blessings. There is no bankruptcy in God. Yes! God sometimes surprises us with great victories that leave us in awe of His goodness. Right now, I am in AWE of His goodness!

The moment you subject yourself to what God wants to do for you by a simple act of obedience, you are positioning yourself for a great blessing.

Abraham obeyed God's instruction as stated in Genesis 12:1, he left his country with his family trusting an all-powerful and all-knowing God to the unknown.

"Now the LORD had said unto Abram, get thee out of thy country, and from thy kindred, and from thy father's house, unto a land that I will show".

God also promised Abraham that he would bless him and make him great, and he will be a blessing.

"And I will make of thee a great nation, and I will bless thee, and make thy name great; and thou shalt be a blessing". (Genesis 12:2)

THERE are moments in my life when God speaks to my heart about doing something and the moment I become hesitant, I realize that I missed out on God's richest blessing. Learning to trust God always comes through an intimate relationship with Him. This is easier said than done. In fact, an intimate relationship would mean that we spend quality time with someone. However, spending time with God in prayer, fasting and in His word is the key to deep intimacy.

As I was thinking about getting a title for this book, the Holy Spirit revealed to me that for me to move into this new phase of my life and where He is taking me, I needed a new mindset. However, I further understood that renewing the mind will cause me to change my lens from fear to faith. What God has for you, requires a higher level of faith. Now is the time to persevere to get there!

Having limited resources and a limited view of the future can leave you wondering if God is able to do what He says He will.

God placed a love for His word deep in my heart, but He also gave me a desire to teach the scriptures to others. My desire was never to study God's Word for myself but to share with everyone. The purpose of your life is not to serve yourselves, but from God's perspective you are here to serve others and to serve Him.

I am absolutely convinced that God is faithful, and He always delivers on His promises. Hebrews 10:23 packs a power verse and it states: *"Hold fast the profession of our faith without waving, for he is faithful that promise"*. You can trust Him to come through for you as you persevere in whatever you do.

We must be willing to persevere to prevail. Things may not look good right now, but you must be willing to go the extra mile with God. I am super excited that God has always remained faithful to his Word. According to Hebrews 13:8 **"He is the same yesterday, today and forever"**

213

Just as I shared with you earlier when talking about Abraham, God instructed him to move forward, and Abraham obeyed based on the fact that the One who was speaking is Faithful.

Your circumstances may be very trying, and you do not know how God will ever gain glory from what you are facing. However, have faith in Him as you reposition yourself to persevere, believe me, YOU WILL GET THERE! EMBRACE YOUR NEW MINDSET!

CONCLUSION

"The LORD hath done great things for us; whereof we are glad". (Psalms 126:3)

It must be emphasized that to maintain a New Mindset requires a renewal of the mind through the Word of God.

"And be not conformed to this world: but be ye transformed by the renewing of your mind, that ye may prove what is that good, and acceptable, and perfect, will of God". (Romans 12:2)

Once your mind is filled with the power of God's truth, your life will be greatly impacted. It is imperative that you maximize your full potential in God, by receiving the promises of God and pursuing purpose.

I am overwhelmingly and irreversibly blessed by this awesome Mind Renewing experience. My mind is renewed, and my life is transformed. Can

215

you imagine all the things to come because of a renewed you?

The Power of the Holy Spirit has expressed Himself on this Journey. I am forever grateful to God for this new move, no longer bound by limitations, rejection, and fear! I have stepped out in **BOLD EXPLOITS.**

To God be the glory!

This move is available to anyone who wants to change their mindset. Know that you are esteemed by God, and you can experience a wealthy mind.

Your mind must be directed to think about things that are right according to God's Word

"Finally, brethren, whatsoever things are true, whatsoever things are honest, whatsoever things are just, whatsoever things are pure, whatsoever things are lovely, whatsoever things are of good report; if there be any virtue, and if there be any praise, think on these things". (Philippians 4: 8)

216

I wholeheartedly encourage you to pursue all of God's purpose for you. Commit yourselves to the continual move to a new mindset.

Accept the freedom that God has given you, knowing that even though you may be imperfect you are still valuable. Thank you, Lord for Restoration of the Breach School and the knowledge gained from the course.

It is never too late to be great. God can use you in spite of your flaws. There is value in your IMPERFECTION.

MIND RENEWAL IS AN INVESTMENT!

Embark on that journey and begin today. You will not regret it! *"This is Lord's doing and it's marvellous in our eyes". (Psalms 118:23)*

POWER SCRIPTURES FOR THE MIND

Romans 12:2

"And be not conformed to this world: but be ye transformed by the renewing of your mind, that ye may prove what is that good, and acceptable, and perfect, will of God".

Philippians 2:5

"Let this mind be in you, which was also in Christ Jesus".

Philippians 4:8

"Finally, brethren, whatsoever things are true, whatsoever things are honest, whatsoever things are just, whatsoever things are pure, whatsoever things are lovely, whatsoever things are of good report; if there be any virtue, and if there be any praise, think on these things".

Isaiah 26:3

"Thou wilt keep him in perfect peace, whose mind is stayed on thee: because he trusteth in thee."

Ephesians 4:23

"And be renewed in the spirit of your mind"

2 Corinthians 10:5

"Casting down imaginations, and every high thing that exalteth itself against the knowledge of God, and bringing into captivity every thought to the obedience of Christ;"

Romans 8:6

"For to be carnally minded is death; but to be spiritually minded is life and peace."

1 Peter 1:13

"Wherefore gird up the loins of your mind, be sober, and hope to the end for the grace that is to be brought unto you at the revelation of Jesus Christ"

Proverbs 23:7

"For as he thinketh in his heart, so is he: Eat and drink, saith he to thee; but his heart is not with thee."

2 Timothy 1:7

"For God hath not given us the spirit of fear; but of power, and of love, and of a sound mind."

ABOUT THE AUTHOR

Jamaican born, Min. Donna Morris is a woman called with purpose and destiny to the kingdom of God for such a time as this.

She has combined twenty (20) years of working in the Life Insurance industry and has garnered a wealth of knowledge. Donna enjoys reading, she loves God's Word and seeks to inspire, encourage and empower others by teaching the scriptures.

221

She is a recent graduate of Whole Life College where she completed courses in Christian Discipleship and Fundamentals in Christian Counselling.

Donna is quick to testify that her journey of Mind Renewal began through Restoration of the Breach School without Borders.

She is a minister and member of The Church of the United Missions Beulah, Kingston Jamaica.

She is a Certified Marriage Master Mentor Relationship Coach from the Institute of Marriage & Family Affairs (TIMFA) USA.

She is married to Deacon Donald Morris, and they are the proud parents of one son, Damari Morris.

MOVED TO A NEW MINDSET is her first of many books.

NOTE: To contact the Author email her at donnamorris431@gmail.com. Kindly submit a review on Amazon or the platform where you bought this book. Thank you.

www.ingramcontent.com/pod-product-compliance
Lightning Source LLC
LaVergne TN
LVHW051228080426
835513LV00016B/1465